Discard 6/12/19

WILDLIFE and PLANTS of the world

An updated and expanded edition of *Wildlife of the World*

now including plants, microorganisms, and biomes

Volume 8

Marshall Cavendish
New York • London • Toronto • Sydney

Marshall Cavendish Corporation
99 White Plains Road
Tarrytown, New York 10591-9001

© Marshall Cavendish Corporation, 1999

Created by **Brown Partworks Ltd**

Library of Congress Cataloging-in-Publication Data

Wildlife and plants of the world.
    p.   cm.
    Includes bibliographical references and index.
    Summary: Alphabetically-arranged illustrated articles introduce over 350 animals, plants, and habitats and efforts to protect them.
    ISBN 0-7614-7099-9 (set : lib. bdg. : alk. paper)
    1. Animals—Juvenile literature. 2. Plants—Juvenile literature.
[1. Animals. 2. Plants.] I. Marshall Cavendish Corporation.
QL49.W539   1998
578—DC21
                        97-32139
                             CIP
                             AC

ISBN 0-7614-7099-9 (set)
ISBN 0-7614-7107-3 (vol.8)

Printed in Malaysia
Bound in the United States

Brown Packaging

Editorial consultants:
- Joshua Ginsberg, Ph.D.
- Jefferey Kaufmann, Ph.D.
- Paul Sieswerda, Ph.D.
(Wildlife Conservation Society)
- Special thanks to the Dept. of Botany,
The Natural History Museum, U.K.

Editors:	Deborah Evans
	Leon Gray
Assistant editor:	Amanda Harman
Art editors:	Joan Curtis
	Alison Gardner
	Sandra Horth
Picture researchers:	Amanda Baker
	Brenda Clynch
Illustrations:	Bill Botten
	John Francis

Marshall Cavendish Corporation

Editorial director:	Paul Bernabeo
Project editor:	Debra M. Jacobs
Editorial consultant:	Elizabeth Kaplan

PICTURE CREDITS

The publishers would like to thank Natural History Photographic Agency, Ardingly, Sussex, U.K., for supplying the following pictures:
Agence Nature 504, 505; A.N.T. (Bruce Thomson) 490, 491; Anthony Bannister 456, 457, 458, 459, 472, 473, 476; Laurie Campbell 482, 507; Stephen Dalton 464, 488, 499; Nigel J. Dennis 466, 471, 503; Robert J. Erwin 480, 481, 484, 486; G.D.T. 461, 474; Ken Griffiths 496; Brian Hawkes 508; E. A. Janes 463; Martin Harvey 469; Daniel Heuclin 502; Tony Howard 478; Hellio & Van Ingen 485; Steven Krasemann 506; Gerard Lacz 475, 492, 493, 510, 511; Trevor McDonald 455; David Middleton 498; Haroldo Palo 470; Peter Parks 454, 477; William S. Paton 465; Peter Pickford 467; Otto Rogge 479; Jany Sauvenet 462; Phillipa Scott 494, 495; John Shaw 500; Eric Soder 460; Alan Williams 487; Norbert Wu 468, 483.

Additional pictures supplied by:
Frank Lane Picture Agency 489, 497, 509.

Front cover
Main image: Jaguar fishing, photographed by Gerard Lacz.
Additional image: Female larch cones, photographed by Laurie Campbell.

Status

In the Key Facts on the species described in this publication, you will find details of the appearance, name (both Latin and common name wherever possible), breeding habits, and so on. The status of an organism indicates how common it is. The status of each organism is based on reference works prepared by two organizations: *1996 IUCN Red List of Threatened Animals* published by the International Union for Conservation of Nature and Natural Resources (IUCN) and *Endangered and Threatened Wildlife and Plants* published in 1997 by the United States Government Printing Office (USGPO)

Extinct:	No sighting in the last 40 years
Endangered:	In danger of becoming extinct
Threatened:	A species that will become endangered if its present condition in the wild continues to deteriorate
Rare:	Not threatened, but not frequently found in the wild
In captivity:	A species that is extinct in the wild but has been kept successfully in captivity
Feral:	Animals that have been domesticated and have escaped into the wild
Common:	Frequently found within its range, which may be limited
Widespread:	Commonly found in many parts of the world

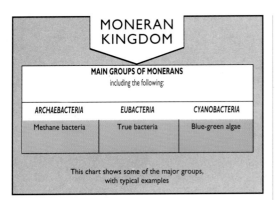

MONERAN KINGDOM

MAIN GROUPS OF MONERANS
including the following:

ARCHAEBACTERIA	EUBACTERIA	CYANOBACTERIA
Methane bacteria	True bacteria	Blue-green algae

This chart shows some of the major groups, with typical examples

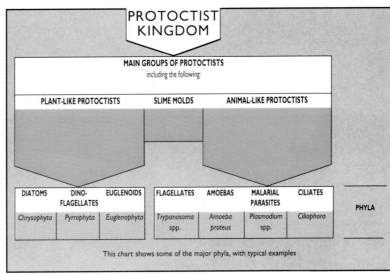

PROTOCTIST KINGDOM

MAIN GROUPS OF PROTOCTISTS
including the following:

PLANT-LIKE PROTOCTISTS			SLIME MOLDS	ANIMAL-LIKE PROTOCTISTS			

DIATOMS	DINO-FLAGELLATES	EUGLENOIDS	FLAGELLATES	AMOEBAS	MALARIAL PARASITES	CILIATES	PHYLA
Chrysophyta	Pyrrophyta	Euglenophyta	Trypanosoma spp.	Amoeba proteus	Plasmodium spp.	Ciliophora	

This chart shows some of the major phyla, with typical examples

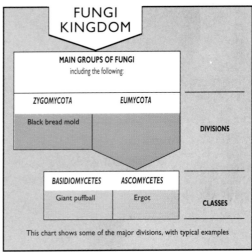

FUNGI KINGDOM

MAIN GROUPS OF FUNGI
including the following:

ZYGOMYCOTA	EUMYCOTA	DIVISIONS
Black bread mold		

BASIDIOMYCETES	ASCOMYCETES	CLASSES
Giant puffball	Ergot	

This chart shows some of the major divisions, with typical examples

Moneran, protoctist, and fungi kingdoms

Three groups of living things are not classified in the animal and plant kingdoms. These are the moneran, protoctist, and fungi kingdoms. Monerans are tiny, single-celled organisms that have no distinct nucleus. The nucleus is the control center of the cell. In contrast, protoctists and fungi have visibly distinct nuclei and tiny organs (called organelles). However, classification is a topic for much debate, and many scientists disagree on the classification of organisms in these three kingdoms.

The moneran kingdom contains all the microscopic, single-celled organisms that do not have distinct nuclei. The three main groups of monerans are: true bacteria, blue-green algae, and methane bacteria. The largest group of monerans is the true bacteria (*Eubacteria*).

For over a billion years, bacteria were the only living things on the earth. Then about 1.5 billion years ago, new organisms, called protoctists (formerly known as protists), evolved from the methane bacteria. All protoctists are single-celled organisms, but their cell structure is more complex than monerans. For example, protoctists have nuclei.

Scientists tend to classify an organism as a protoctist when they cannot place the organism in the animal, plant, or fungi kingdoms. Protoctists are grouped into phyla that have animal-, plant-, or fungus-like features. Single-celled algae, such as diatoms and euglenoids, behave like plants. Amoebas can move about and are more like animals. Slime molds form a subkingdom that have characteristics similar to the fungi kingdom.

Fungi make up the last kingdom of living things. Mushrooms, toadstools, and molds are all fungi. Fungi differ from animals and plants in that they depend on other organisms for their food. Like plants, fungi form groups called divisions. There are two divisions in the fungi kingdom.

See Volume 17 for more information on monerans, protoctists, and fungi.

COLOR GUIDE

MONERANS, PROTOCTISTS, & FUNGI

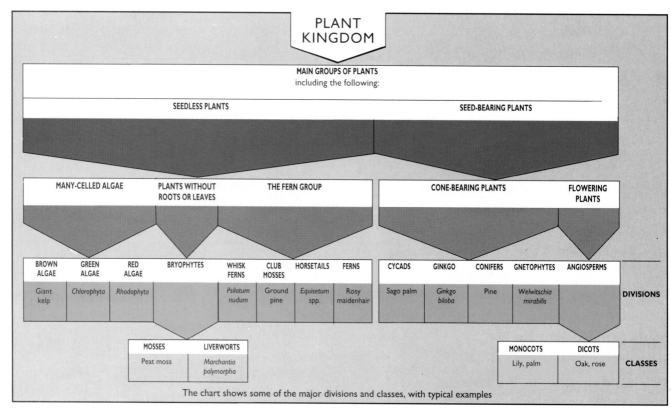

The chart shows some of the major divisions and classes, with typical examples

The plant kingdom

Every plant, from the tiniest shrub to the tallest tree, belongs to the plant kingdom. There are about 500,000 different kinds (species) of plant that have been identified.

The plant kingdom (shown above) can be divided into 13 divisions. A plant division is similar to a phylum in animal classification. Each division represents a number of classes of plants that all have certain features in common.

The simplest plants are algae, all of which live in water. This set of books classifies three divisions of multicellular (or many-celled) algae in the plant kingdom. Some scientists, though, prefer to classify multicellular algae as protoctists.

Two classes, mosses and liverworts, make up the bryophyte division. These plants lack the roots, stems, and leaves that are found in other plant divisions.

The fern group comprises four divisions of the plant kingdom: whisk ferns, club mosses, horsetails, and ferns. All members of the fern group have two stages in their life cycle. During one of these stages tiny reproductive structures, called spores, are released. These spores will eventually grow into a new plant.

More complex plants reproduce with seeds. Four divisions of plants reproduce with "naked" seeds in cones. Cycads, conifers, ginkgoes, and gnetophytes are all cone-bearing plants.

Two classes, monocots and dicots, make up the largest division of plants, the angiosperms, or flowering plants. Unlike cone-bearing plants, angiosperms reproduce with enclosed seeds such as berries, nuts, and fruits.

See Volume 17 for more information on the different divisions of plants.

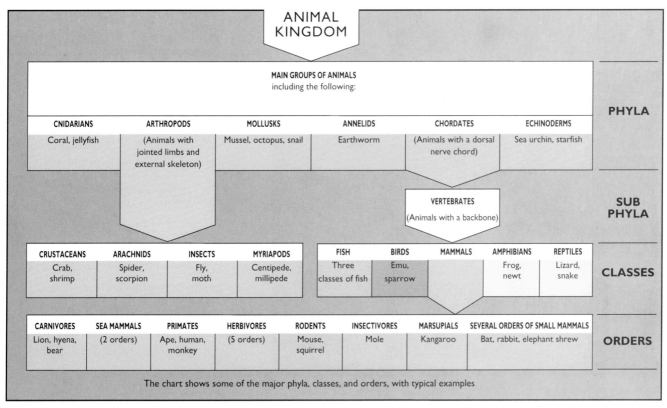

The chart shows some of the major phyla, classes, and orders, with typical examples

Chart contents:

ANIMAL KINGDOM

MAIN GROUPS OF ANIMALS including the following:

PHYLA

CNIDARIANS	ARTHROPODS	MOLLUSKS	ANNELIDS	CHORDATES	ECHINODERMS
Coral, jellyfish	(Animals with jointed limbs and external skeleton)	Mussel, octopus, snail	Earthworm	(Animals with a dorsal nerve chord)	Sea urchin, starfish

SUB PHYLA

VERTEBRATES (Animals with a backbone)

CLASSES

CRUSTACEANS	ARACHNIDS	INSECTS	MYRIAPODS	FISH	BIRDS	MAMMALS	AMPHIBIANS	REPTILES
Crab, shrimp	Spider, scorpion	Fly, moth	Centipede, millipede	Three classes of fish	Emu, sparrow		Frog, newt	Lizard, snake

ORDERS

CARNIVORES	SEA MAMMALS	PRIMATES	HERBIVORES	RODENTS	INSECTIVORES	MARSUPIALS	SEVERAL ORDERS OF SMALL MAMMALS
Lion, hyena, bear	(2 orders)	Ape, human, monkey	(5 orders)	Mouse, squirrel	Mole	Kangaroo	Bat, rabbit, elephant shrew

The animal kingdom

In the eighteenth century, a botanist from Sweden named Carl von Linné (usually known by his Latin name, *Carolus Linneaus*) outlined a system of classifying plants and animals. This became the basis for classification all over the world. Scientists use Latin names so that all plants, animals, and other living things can be identified accurately, even though they have different common names in different places. Linneaus divided living organisms into two kingdoms: plants and animals. Today most scientists divide living things into five kingdoms: animals, plants, monerans, protoctists, and fungi. The animal kingdom (*above*) is divided into many phyla. Most of the phyla of the animal kingdom contain strange creatures – microscopic organisms, sponges, corals, slugs, and insects – without the backbone and central nervous system that we associate with more familiar animals.

Each phylum is divided into classes. For example, vertebrates (animals with a backbone) are a subdivision of a phylum and are divided up into seven classes: mammals, birds, reptiles, amphibians, and three classes of fish (represented by eels, sharks, and trout).

Each of these classes is broken down further into different orders. The mammal class, for instance, includes the orders carnivores (meat eaters), insectivores (insect eaters), primates (monkeys, apes), and marsupials (kangaroos, koalas), among others.

In this set of books, we give Latin names for different groups (genera) and kinds (species) of animals. See Volume 17 for more information on the different phyla of animals.

COLOR GUIDE

INVERTEBRATES

FISH

AMPHIBIANS & REPTILES

BIRDS

MAMMALS

PLANTS

BIOMES & HABITATS

MONERANS, PROTOCTISTS, & FUNGI

Hydra

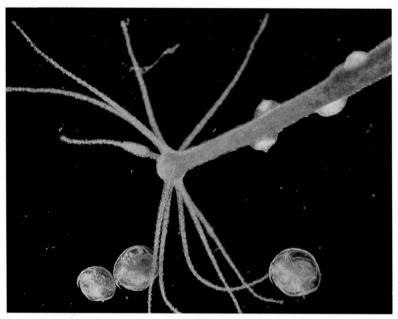

Imagine an invertebrate (spineless animal) so simple that all it consists of is a hollow tube or stalk, with a circle of tentacles and a mouth at one end. Believe it or not, your imaginary creature is a real animal called a hydra, which is related to the jellyfish and the sea anemones. Unlike these marine relatives, hydras are freshwater animals. There are between 20 to 30 species in the group (genus) *Hydra*. These meat-eating animals (carnivores) are found in lakes, ponds, rivers, and streams around the world. Ten of the hydra species occur in North America.

A large family

Corals, hydras, jellyfish, and sea anemones all belong to the phylum *Cnidaria* (formerly known as the phylum *Coelenterata*). There are about 9000 living members in this phylum, and they have evolved into three groups called classes.

▲ *This hydra (***Hydra viridis***) has captured prey on its tentacles. The tentacles contain stinging cells that make the victim unable to move. The strength of the venom contained within these cells varies from species to species. Only some hydras kill their prey – other hydras can only subdue their prey. Hydras also use the stinging cells as a form of defense against predators such as small fish and meat-eating (carnivorous) water insects.*

The hydras belong to a class called the *Hydrozoa,* or "hydra-like animals," which contains over 2700 species. Many of these, such as species from the genus *Hydractinia,* look like hydras but tend to live together in small groups called colonies. Within a colony, which may measure just 2 in (5 cm) across, individuals have different functions, such as feeding, protection, and reproduction. One familiar creature from the class *Hydrozoa* is the Portuguese man-of-war (*Physalia* spp.), which is often mistaken for a jellyfish. This well-known creature floats in seawater, catching and killing fish with its long, dangling tentacles, which may reach up to 90 ft (30 m) in length.

A solitary lifestyle

Hydras are very similar to coral polyps. Unlike those colonial animals, hydras prefer to live a solitary life. Many hydras are translucent (almost clear), while others appear brown, green, or white in color. They are very small, rarely reaching more than 1 in (2.5 cm) in length.

Most hydras are sedentary (unmoving). They attach themselves to underwater plants or rocks in a lake or riverbed by secreting a sticky mucus from their base. However, some can move, either by creeping along very slowly on the base of their stalk or by looping. When looping, the hydra grabs hold of something with its tentacles, unsticks its base, and somersaults "head-over-heels" until the base attaches to a new surface.

Stinging tentacles

Hydras have extremely sensitive skin. If touched, they will shrink away (contract). This reflex offers some protection from predators such as small fish or carnivorous water insects. If the hydra is attacked and injured badly, it is able to regenerate (regrow) new body parts such as tentacles, or even whole new individuals.

However, these animals have another defense. Like most jellyfish and sea anemones, hydras can sting their enemies. Some hydras have long, harpoon-like, venomous barbs on springs in their tentacles. If the springs are triggered, the barbs puncture the victim's skin and enter its body, numbing it completely.

During feeding, hydras also use their stinging weapons to subdue their prey, such as aquatic worms, small crustaceans, tadpoles, or insect larvae. Once they have stung their prey, the tentacles — which usually number between four and eight — draw it rapidly into the hydra's mouth and down into its stomach to be digested.

Baby hydras

Hydras reproduce in several ways. The simplest is budding, in which tiny versions of the adult develop on the side of the tube. They separate from the base of their stalk to become new individuals. When the hydras are well fed, budding can occur at any time of year, every few days or so. During the fall and early winter, however, sexual reproduction takes place. Some species of hydra have individuals of different sexes. Other species are hermaphrodites and have male and female sexual characteristics in the same individual. When hydra eggs have been fertilized by male sperm, a tiny embryo develops in a protective sac on the outside of the parent. Eventually this embryo breaks free and develops further during the winter. It hatches as a small hydra in the spring.

KEY FACTS

● **Name**
Hydra (*Hydra* spp.)

● **Range**
Worldwide

● **Habitat**
Freshwater lakes, ponds, rivers, and streams

● **Appearance**
Small creatures, about 1 in (2.5 cm) long; appear brown, green, white, or almost clear; a hollow tube, attached to plants or rocks at the base, with a mouth at one end and four to eight stinging tentacles at the other end

● **Food**
Small crustaceans, tadpoles, worms, and insect larvae

● **Breeding**
Budding or sexual reproduction, usually by hermaphrodites

● **Status**
Widespread

◀ *These hydrozoans (Lytocarpia nuttingi), from the Sea of Cortez, Mexico, have attached themselves to the ocean floor by secreting a sticky mucus from their base.*

See also **Coral; Jellyfish; Lake, river, and estuary; Sea anemone**

Hyena

Hyenas have a bad reputation. They are often considered to be scavengers, stealing food from other predators such as lions, cheetahs, or wild dogs. Although hyenas do steal carcasses, they kill the vast majority of the food they eat. Not only are they efficient killers, but to a hyena, a wasted scrap is unheard of. Their coats are mottled beige and brown, providing good cover in the dry grasslands. In the case of the Spotted hyena, the markings are irregularly sized blotches, whereas other species are predominantly striped.

Hunters in the dark

Hunting mainly at night, hyenas are extremely flexible in their hunting strategies. When large prey are rare they will hunt smaller gazelles, rodents, tortoises, or pangolins. But they are extremely skilled in hunting in groups and can take down animals as large as buffalo, zebras, small rhinoceroses, or young hippos. They use their characteristic call,

▲ *The hunched shoulders of a hyena give it a rather sulky look. Its great strength is in these shoulders, where the muscle creates a high, arched back.*

a long whooping sound, to keep in contact during a hunt. Well-organized packs of hyenas even challenge lions for their prey. They have little to fear from large cats or other predators that live in the same area.

Hyenas have evolved to make the most of their kills. Their jaws are lined with flat, square, strong back teeth, capable of crushing bones and sharp enough to rip tendon and sinew. The muscles that run from their forehead to their jaws (the *maseeter* and *temporalis* muscles) are enormous, providing tremendous force to the jaw. Their jaws are so strong that they have been known to eat tires off a parked car! Their digestive systems are also extremely efficient and dissolve most of what they eat – including fur and bone.

Females first

Hyenas live in large, extended families called clans, with up to 50 animals sharing a denning area. Unlike most animals, female hyenas are larger than males, and females dominate males in all aspects of social life. The social life of the hyena is highly structured, with families of sisters, aunts, and female cousins all living in the clan. Each adult female produces two or three young each year and related females will often help rear each other's young. The young are nursed for up to eight months – unusually long for a carnivore.

Female hyenas look like males. Before they are born, baby hyenas are exposed to very high doses of chemicals normally only present in males: the male hormone, testosterone. This results in female sexual organs that look almost exactly like those of males. These high doses of testosterone also result in very aggressive young.

Tough cubs

Baby hyenas are born with their canines or "dog teeth." Scientists knew that the young hyenas lived only on milk and did not need teeth for eating, and for many years they thought they used their teeth to defend themselves. The real story is much more gruesome. Within the hyena clan, dominance is determined by size. Size, in turn, is determined by how much food a baby gets from its mother. If a young hyena kills a littermate, it gets more food, grows bigger, and is dominant in the clan. The teeth hyenas are born with, and the agressive nature they get from large doses of male hormones, enable the young hyenas to kill their weaker littermates.

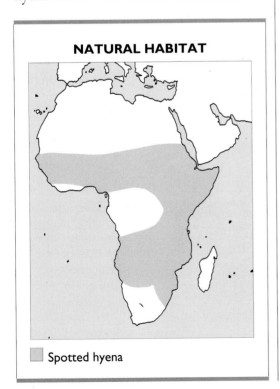

NATURAL HABITAT

Spotted hyena

▲ *Young hyenas stay with their mother for several months after birth, and her milk is the mainstay of their diet for about 8 months.*

Such behavior is seen in many birds, but is extremely unusual in mammals.

Hyenas are feared by people, but attacks by hyenas on humans are extremely rare. Occasionally, hyenas kill sheep and cattle, but such events are not as common as some people think. Hyenas can be beneficial as they are natural garbage disposers, scavenging dead animals and garbage in areas around human habitation. Nonetheless, many countries still have active campaigns against hyenas. Because they will so readily scavenge a dead carcass, poisoning is an effective and deadly way to eliminate hyenas.

In addition to the Spotted hyena, there are two other species, the Brown and the Striped hyenas. Both are nocturnal. The Brown hyena is found only in the deserts and woodlands of southern Africa. Mainly a scavenger, it also eats small mammals, birds, fruit, and insects. The Striped hyena was once found in southern Europe but now only exists in North Africa, the Middle East, and parts of India.

KEY FACTS

● **Name**
Spotted hyena
(*Crocuta crocuta*)

● **Range**
Savannah belt of western and central Africa, throughout eastern and parts of southern Africa

● **Habitat**
Open plains and woodlands, but not true forests

● **Appearance**
A dog-like face with small, rounded ears and a large forehead; strong muscles in the shoulders; short hind legs that make the back slope downward; a distinctive spotted coat, brown on a beige background

● **Food**
Freshly killed hoofed mammals, but also scavenges and steals kills from others

● **Breeding**
Live in large, female-dominated clans; each female produces 1-3 young a year after a gestation of nearly 4 months

● **Status**
Common in some areas, but widely persecuted through poisoning campaigns

See also **African wild dog**

Hyrax

Hanging in a small tree or bush, or scampering over the rocky outcrops of central and southern Africa, hyraxes look very much like large rodents, perhaps squirrels. Their long, chunky bodies, small heads and ears, and their constantly growing front teeth are also rodent-like. Given these similarities, it often comes as a surprise to people that the closest relative of the hyrax is, in fact, the elephant! Elephants, dugongs, and hyraxes all shared an ancestor some 60 million years ago. Since then, of course, they have all developed in quite different ways.

The relatively close family links with elephants and other hoofed animals, although not obvious from their size, are seen in the way hyraxes breed. Although adult hyraxes weigh under 10 lb (4.5 kg), they have a gestation period that is seven months – more than double what one would expect. When the young are born they are very highly developed, but their mothers continue to nurse them for up to five months. For comparison, this would be like a woman being pregnant for 20 months and breastfeeding for three years.

Rock lovers

The best known of the hyraxes are the four species of rock hyraxes, also known as dassies. Rock hyraxes all share a similar

▼ *These Cape rock hyraxes seem to have few predators on the rocky coastal shore. They huddle together for warmth in the evening sun.*

KEY FACTS

● **Name**
Cape rock hyrax or dassie
(*Procavia capensis*)

● **Range**
Most of Africa and into Asia

● **Habitat**
Almost any rocky habitat, from deserts to mountains, including coasts

● **Appearance**
17-18 in (43-46 cm) long; a tube-shaped body, short neck and a small head with small ears; the sharp and curling front teeth look like those of a porcupine; short, coarse hair which varies in color with location, from black to light brown

● **Food**
Fine green grass, berries, fruit, leaves

● **Breeding**
Extremely long (7 month) gestation period; each female produces 1 to 4 young each year, nursing them for 4-5 months

● **Status**
Common

social system. They live in unusually large social groups with up to five to seven females and their young, a dominant or territorial male, and sometimes young nonbreeding males. Each female raises her own young, although the females join together to protect the young from predators. At about 18 months, males leave the territory in which they are born and move to new groups. Because the rocky areas in which they live are often far apart, many young males die during the move. Like many primate species, young females stay in the group in which they were born for their entire lives.

Scent marking

Hyraxes will vigorously defend their territories from intruders, although such active defense is rarely needed. Using oil glands on their hindquarters, hyraxes mark their territorial boundaries with a strong

smelling musky oil. These marks tell any creature that enters the territory that a rock pile is already occupied.

Scent glands may also serve to bond a hyrax group together. In the night, when the hyraxes are sleeping, they often come together in dark holes or cracks in the rock and pile up one on top of another in a heap. Other animals, including pet gerbils, also do this.

Two explanations have been given for this heaping behavior. The first is very straightforward. Although hyraxes live in Africa, the nights can be very cold indeed, with temperatures as low as 30 or 40°F (0-4°C). By piling up together, the hyraxes keep warm. The piles, however, also result in each hyrax rubbing up against other hyraxes and exchanging scent, perhaps to make a communal smell that identifies the group.

▲ *If a hyrax feels threatened by a predator (or a photographer!) it will bare its teeth and growl in much the same way as a dog. However, these creatures are much smaller than dogs and look rather like large rabbits with short ears.*

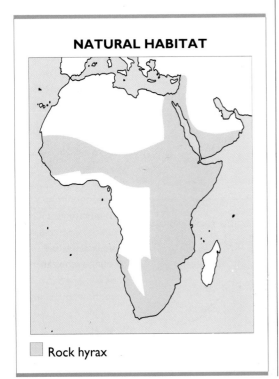

NATURAL HABITAT

☐ Rock hyrax

See also **Elephant**

Ibex

The ibex is a large mountain goat that is found on the highest mountaintops, above the tree line where little else survives. Like other mountain goats, it is successful because it is able to specialize in a habitat so severe and inhospitable that almost no other animal can compete with it.

Keeping warm

The ibex has adapted well to this extreme environment. Its shaggy brown coat acts as insulation, keeping the ibex warm even in sub-zero temperatures. Its hoofs, like those of many mountain goats, can support the entire animal as it picks its way across the rock face. Its diet is varied, and it eats almost any vegetation that it can find – roots, shoots, leaves, and grass are all eaten and digested efficiently.

▲ *These bucks are competing for mates during the breeding season, using their huge horns as powerful battle weapons while others look on.*

In the summer months, food on the mountaintops is plentiful, but when the winter arrives with heavy snow, the ibex must work harder for its dinner. In some areas, ibex scamper along windswept cliffs, finding grass and shrubs exposed by the wind. However, in other areas, they use their feet to dig the buried food out from under the snow. Their sense of smell is keen – the ibex will dig away up to a foot (30 cm) of snow if it detects buried acorns, a rich source of energy in the frozen landscape.

Competition for mates among ibex is severe. This competition has led to three

KEY FACTS

● **Name**
Ibex (*Capra ibex*)

● **Range**
Mongolia and central China, through Afghanistan, the Arabian peninsula, and south to northern Ethiopia

● **Habitat**
High altitude meadows and rocky outcrops above the timberline (the highest altitude at which trees occur)

● **Appearance**
A majestic beast, measuring up to 5 ft (1.5 m) and weighing as much as 240 lb (110 kg); massive, thick horns arching over its head; an even, dark brown coat; a small "beard" on the chin

● **Food**
Grasses, reeds, and the leaves of shrubs

● **Breeding**
Intense competition among males for mates; females bear a single young 5 months after mating

● **Status**
Rare in some areas

▶ *After mating is over, large male ibex stay with a herd of females. Indeed, this behavior is more common in goats than in their close cousins, the sheep. The group structure of ibex is very flexible, with animals leaving and joining herds as they search the mountaintops for food. Ibex, unlike many animals, do not have territories that they defend from competitors, but wander widely and freely, with larger males using their size to defend the females in their herd rather than a territory.*

distinctive characteristics in male ibex: a large body, large horns, and incredibly nimble feet. When females are ready to breed, males try to defend them. The larger the male, the more aggressive he becomes during the breeding season.

A large, dominant male will chase smaller males across the slippery slopes and rocky crags of the high mountains, physically removing them from their breeding areas. When large competitors show up, however, males must engage in dangerous battles. Two large males charge each other, slamming their heads and horns

together in a massive clash. These fights can lead to death but, more often than not, the losing male turns around and sticks his rump in the victor's face, a clear sign of submission in many animals.

Owned by humans?

Humans have domesticated many goat-like animals. In fact, the origins of our domestic goats are uncertain, and some scientists think they may have come about as a mix of several wild species. For years no one thought that the independent and mountain loving ibex could ever have been domesticated by humans. The discovery of ancient hieroglyphics or rock carvings has changed this theory. It seems that thousands of years ago, the ancient Egyptians captured and kept ibex. These animals may have been used as farm animals, or they may just have been kept in ancient zoos — no one is certain.

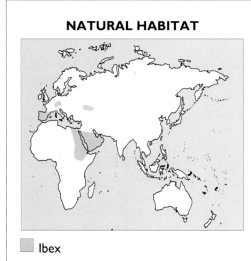

NATURAL HABITAT

Ibex

See also **Goat**

Ibis

The ibis is a bird with a long history. The Ancient Egyptians worshipped the Sacred ibis (*Threskiornis aethiopicus*), which was believed to be the animal form of Thoth, the god of wisdom and magic. Ibises were often mummified and buried in temples with their pharaohs. In Egypt the Sacred ibis has now been extinct for nearly 100 years, but it is still common in Africa south of the Sahara.

Ibises are elegant wading birds, with sleek feathers and long legs, and they seem to enjoy each other's company as well as the company of other birds. There are some 27 different species of ibis thoughout the world, all living in tropical and warm temperate zones.

Flocking to water

Most ibises live and feed in shallow freshwater lakes, marshes, and swamps:

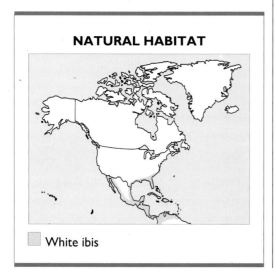

NATURAL HABITAT

☐ White ibis

▲ *Scarlet ibises are a startling sight, perched in the treetops in large groups. They are native to South America, but are accidental visitors to southern Florida and the Texas coast. The first ibises to nest in the states (the White, White-faced, and Glossy ibises) arrived at the end of the nineteenth century and have successfully moved northward.*

KEY FACTS

● **Name**
White ibis
(*Eudocimus albus*)

● **Range**
South Carolina to
Texas, Mexico,
Central America,
parts of Caribbean

● **Habitat**
Marshes and swamps

● **Appearance**
22-24 in (55-58 cm)
mainly white with
red legs; bill is red,
downward-curving

● **Food**
Invertebrates:
insects, crustaceans

● **Breeding**
In colonies, usually
with herons and
other large waders;
the nest is built by
both parents and is a
platform of sticks in
trees, especially
mangroves; 3-4 eggs
are laid March-Aug
and incubated for 21
days by both parents;
the chicks are fed
regurgitated food

● **Status**
Common

▶ *The White ibis is
becoming more
common in eastern
North America where
it is protected by law.*

they are found on flooded farmland and in some parts of the world they move onto the rice fields. They have long legs and downward-curving beaks that are perfect for stalking through the water and probing the bottom for food. Ibises also have partly webbed toes to help spread their weight as they stalk through the mud.

Rather than use their eyesight to catch their prey, they use their beaks to probe for it, catching small crustaceans, fish, and insects, as well as larvae and frogs. Ibises that live away from water catch beetles, ants, grasshoppers, reptiles, and sometimes eat carrion, eggs, or even small rodents.

Nesting time

Ibises can be seen in large groups, feeding together and making grunting calls to each other as they feed. At breeding time they form colonies, often mixing with other species of wading birds. The birds pair up each season, working together to build an untidy nest of sticks and twigs. Most ibises choose low trees near wetlands, but sometimes they nest on cliffs and rocky outcrops. Some species build their nests on the ground. There is often a display at the nesting site, with pairs of birds bowing and stretching their necks forward.

Both male and female care for the eggs: there are usually between two and five, and they have to be tended for nearly a month. After hatching, it is a month before the nestlings learn the strong flight techniques of their parents; it is three years before they are regarded as adults.

The numbers of ibises have dropped in many parts of the world, and two species, the Japanese crested ibis and Northern bald ibis, are endangered. All species of ibis found in North America (either permanent residents or occasional visitors) are protected by law.

Iguana

◀ *The Common iguana of Central and South America has leathery skin and spines down its back.*

KEY FACTS

● **Name**
Marine iguana
(*Amblyrhynchus cristatus*)

● **Range**
Galapagos Islands

● **Habitat**
Coastal rocks

● **Appearance**
4-5 ft (1.2-1.5 m) long; red, brown, and black tortoiseshell effect; darker legs, spines over the head and backbone; a long tail; five toes on each foot, with claws

● **Food**
Seaweed and algae

● **Breeding**
Males defend the territory and fight for the females; the female lays 2 or 3 eggs in a sandy hole; the young often stay together for defense

● **Status**
Threatened

NATURAL HABITAT

■ Marine iguana

Iguanas are a large family of lizards, most of which live in North, Central, and South America and the outlying islands. Members of the iguana family are also found in Madagascar and Fiji. There are over 600 different species of iguana altogether, of which 17 species or subspecies are threatened or endangered.

The species that are in greatest danger of dying out are those that live on islands. For millions of years, these species were able to live peacefully because there were few mammals to trouble them. However, in the Caribbean and in Fiji, the introduction of the mongoose, as well as domestic dogs, cats, goats, and cattle, have restricted the numbers of iguanas.

The Common iguana of northern South and Central America is a tree-dwelling lizard that lives near water. It is the giant of the family; it may grow up to 6½ ft (2 m) long. It is green in color with black rings on its tail and spines all down its back. It has been introduced into the southern states, particularly Florida. Although they are not meat eaters, they will fight other animals if they are attacked and can be quite fierce.

Seaside lizards

The most individual member of the iguana family is the Marine iguana. This creature is found only on the Galapagos Islands, on the equator off the coast of Ecuador. The Marine iguana is the only lizard that goes into salty seawater: it feeds on seaweed and algae. The sea gives it a plentiful supply of water, but in order to cope with the salty seawater it has special glands that remove excess salt from its food. It sprays this salt out through its nose with a cloud of tiny water droplets.

Once in the water, the Marine iguana either swims or walks on the bottom. It cannot breathe under water, but its heart rate slows down so that it can stay under the surface for a long time. As it swims, it uses its tail to propel itself through the water, and it uses its feet to steer.

Male Marine iguanas become territorial at the start of the mating season, fighting with other males. The fight is more of a ritual than an all-out battle, with head butting and clawing but no serious injuries. Once a fight is over, the intruder does not usually come back to fight again but retires to find another territory. The larger males establish the largest territories and mate with more females.

After mating, the female digs a shallow hole in the sand on the beach and lays two or three eggs. The ground is warm and the eggs well enough protected for them to be left to incubate without any attention from the mother, and they hatch after some three or four months. After hatching, Marine iguanas (and many other species of iguana) often live in groups with one acting as leader. If the mother has a second brood, the newly hatched lizards may form a group with the older ones, all on the lookout for predators.

Other species

Besides the huge Common and Marine iguanas, there are many smaller species that are found in North America. The Eastern fence lizard (*Sceloporus undulatus*) is found down the east coast, from Virginia to Florida, and across to Mexico. The spiny Texas horned lizard (*Phrynosoma cornutum*), with its flattened, armor-plated body, is found from Kansas to Texas and Arizona. The Chuckwalla (*Souromalus obesus*) is a desert species found in Nevada, Southern California, Utah, Arizona, and Mexico.

▼ *Young Marine iguanas usually form well-organized groups. They have been seen to groom and rub against each other and may huddle together for protection at night.*

See also **Alga, Kelp and other seaweeds**

Impala

Throughout southern and eastern Africa, in many habitats, one of the most frequently seen antelopes is the impala. The impala is an exceptionally graceful and beautiful animal. With long legs and a short, compact body, this medium-sized antelope is like an art student's study in color. It starts with a band of rich reddish-

▲ *A male impala drinks from a pool of water in the warm evening light; its elegant horns add to the graceful silhouette of this antelope.*

brown across the back and top of the flanks, followed by a creamy coffee color across the flanks and face, and ends in a pure or creamy white belly. Only the male impala have horns. The horns grow larger with age, starting first as spikes and, in subsequent years, growing longer until they arch over the head in graceful curves.

Water in the diet

Impala are not found everywhere and they avoid both dense forests where no grass can grow and open plains with little bush cover. Where they are found, however, they are often extremely common. This is due, in part, to their broad tastes in food. Most hoofed animals, or ungulates, eat either grass (grazers) or bushes and trees (browsers). The impala is a jack-of-all-

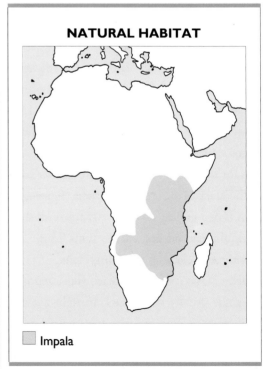

NATURAL HABITAT

☐ Impala

trades and will eat any green vegetation it can find. Impala must drink every day, so a source of drinking water is essential in their habitat.

Breeding in the impala is fast and furious. Most births in southern African impala occur just before the rains in May and June, about 6¹/₂ months after mating. Before the breeding season, large dominant males set up breeding territories, roaring to attract up to 20 females and to repel competitors. Because the breeding season is so intense and short, males stop eating during this time.

Plentiful and tasty

The strict season for breeding and births has developed for two reasons. The first is to take advantage of the green grass that sprouts with the first of the rains. The second and perhaps most important reason is that impala are the favorite food of many predators. Leopards, cheetahs, African wild dogs, jackals, lions, even baboons find young impala a tasty treat — easy to catch and delicious. If the young

▲ *When alarmed, impala flee through grass and scrub with an amazingly high, bounding stride. Their main enemies are big cats and wild dogs.*

were born throughout the year, the predators would pick them off one by one when they were most vulnerable. By giving birth all at the same time, the impala "flood" the predators with food. Even if they eat as much as they can catch, the predators cannot make a dent in the huge population of young impala. By the time the young impala lambs are five or six months old, many young have avoided being eaten and are larger and much harder to catch.

Three subspecies have been identified: the southern race (*Aepyceros melampus melampus*) in southern Congo, south to Zimbabwe and South Africa, and west to Botswana; *A. m. rendilis*, in northern Kenya, Uganda, and Tanzania; and the Angolan impala, *A. m. petersi*, also known as the Black-faced impala. The Black-faced impala may be threatened due to its relatively restricted distribution.

Island

What do you think of when you imagine an island? Probably a small patch of land surrounded by sea, with golden beaches and palm trees. Biologists, however, have a much broader definition. To them, an island is any small area that is surrounded by a different type of environment. For example, a nature reserve is an island to a biologist. In this article, however, we will consider only oceanic islands.

Island transport

Because they are so isolated, islands are difficult to get to for many animals. Some, such as insects, reptiles, and small rodents, arrive accidentally after being transported across the ocean on floating vegetation or ships. Others, such as small birds, get blown off course by strong winds during migration and end up making islands their home. For seabirds, traveling to and from islands is not such a difficult thing. Once they arrive, many stay because the ocean around the island is a rich source of food.

Even some plants do not have a problem reaching island habitats. Their seeds may be introduced by birds, either in their droppings or stuck to their feet and feathers. Some seeds are so light they can

▲ *This coral island formed when rocks and other material accumulated on top of the coral reef in a shoal. More deposits were added to the shoal by waves, and beaches of coral sand developed around it.*

AN ISLAND HABITAT

Hawaiian Islands

be carried on the breeze for many miles. Still others, such as the coconut, reach islands by floating across the sea.

Unique species

In general, larger islands and islands closer to the mainland have more species than smaller islands and islands farther from the mainland. Animals and plants that inhabit smaller and more isolated islands are often unique, existing nowhere else in the world. Over time, these animals and plants have become so isolated from their relatives on the mainland that they have changed into new species. This process of change is known as evolution.

Diversification

When an animal first reaches an island it may find very few competitors for food, water, and space. It can exploit all the resources for itself and grow to a much larger size than it would normally back on the mainland. For example, the Komodo dragon (*Varanus komodoensis*), which is found on the island of Komodo in Indonesia, may reach 10 ft (3 m) long. This is much bigger than other closely related lizards. On some islands, however, the opposite has happened. Limited food supplies have resulted in smaller species, such as the Pygmy rattlesnake found on islands in the Sea of Cortez near Mexico.

Darwin's finches

Several species of finches – collectively called Darwin's finches – live on the Galápagos Islands near South America. These birds have evolved different shaped beaks, reflecting the type of food available on the different islands. On one island, smaller species of finch have more delicate beaks, allowing them to eat only small seeds. On another island, however, the finches have larger beaks, enabling them to crack open the hard fruits of the Caltrop bush (*Tribulus cistoides*) that grows there.

A safe haven?

Unless species are able to fly, oceans may prevent most ground-dwelling and freshwater animals from reaching islands. One of the advantages of this, from an island inhabitant's point of view, is that there are usually no large predators. As a result, many animals slowly lose the ability to escape from their enemies. Some island birds, such as the kiwi (*Apteryx* spp.) and the kakapo (*Strigops habroptilus*) of New Zealand, have lost the ability to fly. One of the main reasons for flight – to escape from predators – is an unnecessary luxury if the island has no predators. However, this also means these animals are extremely vulnerable if meat-eating animals are introduced to their home (usually by humans). Even a single domestic cat can wipe out an entire population of birds. This is exactly what happened to the tiny Flightless wren (*Xenicus lyalli*) on Stephen Island, near New Zealand, in 1894. Humans have been responsible for the disappearance of many island animals in other ways, too. The most famous of these is the dodo (*Raphus cucullatus*) from Mauritius in the Indian Ocean, which was hunted to extinction during the seventeenth century.

◀ *The fierce-looking Komodo dragon lives in Indonesia.*

KEY FACTS

- **What is an island?**
  Any isolated area that is surrounded by a completely different kind of environment

- **Origins of oceanic islands**
  Various – some islands are created by underwater volcanoes, others are created by corals, still others are created when the sea level rises and cuts off pieces of land from the mainland

- **Examples of oceanic islands**
  Galápagos Islands (Pacific Ocean), Hawaiian Islands (Pacific Ocean), Madagascar (Indian Ocean), Maldives (Indian Ocean), Mauritius (Indian Ocean), South Sea Islands (Pacific Ocean)

- **Typical island inhabitants**
  Coconut palms, chameleons, crabs, finches, Frigate birds, Giant tortoises, iguanas, kakapos, kiwis, Komodo dragons, lemurs, parrots, seals

---

See also **Coconut palm, Coral reef, Kiwi, Komodo dragon, Palm**

Jacana

▲ *The Northern jacana has a long slim body and long legs that are well adapted to its habitat of reeds and grasses along the water's edge. Here it spends its days searching for insects to eat and occasionally catching small or larval fish.*

Jacanas are small waders that look rather like gallinules, or moorhens. Their most striking characteristic is the length of their toes and claws, which enables them to walk on top of floating plants. The way that they walk on the leaves of water lilies gives them the nickname "Lily-trotter." Most have a fleshy shield above the bill, similar to that of a coot. Jacanas are generally more colorful than Common coots and American gallinules: they have feathers in tones of cinnamon, yellow, white, and dark brown or black.

Jacanas are found in many parts of the world: in marshlands, rice fields, along rivers, and near freshwater lakes in tropical and semitropical regions. There are eight species altogether, of which only one is found in North America. This is the Northern Jacana that lives in Central America and occasionally ventures into Texas and the southern states.

They eat a mixed diet of insects (particularly those that live in water), mollusks, and the occasional small fish. They also eat the seeds of reeds and other water plants.

Tropical trotters

As they search for their food they stalk nimbly from leaf to leaf, occasionally jumping a patch of water with the help of a flick of their wings. As they land, they have the habit of raising their wings so that they almost meet over their backs. This movement shows off the paler colored feathers under the wings and the spurs (like sharp claws) on the leading edge of their wings. These spurs are used to defend their territories during the breeding season. It is possible to approach

NATURAL HABITAT

Northern jacana

jacanas quite closely without alarming them. However, if they are frightened by a large bird or other animal, they stand motionless and become very difficult to see amongst the reeds in spite of their quite strong coloring.

Role reversal

The breeding season for most jacanas is during the wettest part of the year when insects are plentiful. The Northern jacana, which lives mainly in Central America, lays its eggs between April and August in most parts of Mexico, or between January and October in Costa Rica.

The most remarkable feature of the jacana is its unusual breeding pattern. The female jacana (which is larger than the male) usually establishes a territory. Within that territory there may be three or four males with whom she mates. The males are the nest builders and, after the female has laid her eggs, the males look after the eggs and rear the young. The nest itself is a mass of floating twigs and leaves, and sometimes it drifts over ponds and swamps.

Once the eggs have hatched, the male feeds and protects the chicks. In heavy rains the male takes the chicks under its wing to provide shelter. The chicks take three or four months to develop enough to leave the protection of their father. The female is thought to visit her mate regularly in the breeding season.

▼ *Jacanas are found in tropical and subtropical regions. This African jacana has strong blue coloring on the front of its head. It is the male that builds the floating nest and tends the eggs.*

KEY FACTS

- **Name**
Northern
(or American) jacana
(*Jacana spinosa*)

- **Range**
Central America and the Caribbean; a rare visitor to Texas

- **Habitat**
Aquatic habitats

- **Appearance**
8-9 in (20-22 cm) long; the female is larger than the male; a yellow bill, a forehead with a red and yellow frontal shield; the head, neck, chest, and upper back are glossy black, elsewhere is a deep chestnut or maroon; greenish-yellow flight feathers

- **Food**
Mainly insects; some small fish

- **Breeding**
Female has the territory with 1-4 smaller males; the nest is built by the male; green leaves on a floating mat of plants, built up to stop the eggs from rolling out; usually 4, almost round eggs; the male incubates them for 22-24 days

- **Status**
Widespread

See also **Coot, Crane, Gallinule**

Jackal

◄ *The Black-backed jackal of southwestern Africa is a small jackal with distinctive black and silver fur covering its back. The male defends its territory fiercely against other males, while females try to chase away any female intruders. Young jackals may stay with their parents for several years, playing and having mock battles with each other, until they are old enough to leave the family group.*

There are only four species of jackal, yet jackals are at the same time among the most common and among the rarest animals in the world. The Black-backed (or Silver-backed) jackal is common in the plains and woodlands of eastern and southern Africa. The Golden jackal, found in Africa and east Asia, is also common and expanding its range. The Side-striped jackal, with a white stripe on its side, is common in central and southern Africa. Yet the Simien jackal is becoming very rare. Found only in the highland mountain meadows of Ethiopia, perhaps only 350 of these elegant brown-backed, white-bellied, large dog-like animals remain. Disease, habitat loss, and years of war have all contributed to the near loss of this species.

Not so nasty

Jackals, like their cousins the foxes, dogs, and other wolf-like animals, are often looked upon with distaste. They are thought to be scavengers of dead, rotting carcasses, or carriers of fatal diseases like rabies. To call someone a jackal is not a compliment but an insult. Yet jackals are harmless and very playful animals, good parents, and keen hunters. Although

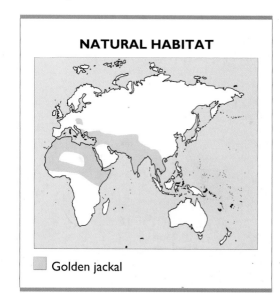

NATURAL HABITAT

Golden jackal

they sometimes try to steal meat off the carcass of an animal killed by a lion or hyena, most of their diet consists of seeds, fruit, insects, and small mammals. Jackals are particularly fond of mice and rats, and one pair of jackals can eat hundreds, if not thousands, of cane rats in a year. Not surprisingly, jackals play an important part in maintaining the natural balance in many parts of Africa, helping to keep rodent pest numbers low.

Puppy love

Male, or dog, jackals usually pair up with a female, known as a bitch. This family group lives on a small territory of around 110-550 acres (45-223 hectares). The breeding season varies by species, but is often timed to coincide with the time of year in which food is plentiful. Two

months after mating, three or four puppies are born to the family pair. The puppies remain underground in a den for three or four weeks. The den is a safe shelter from the weather and, more importantly, from predators such as eagles, hawks, hyenas, and lions.

The pups are fed on milk by the mother for a short time, approximately eight to ten weeks, and then move on to solid food. Males provide at least half the food for the puppies. The pups reach sexual maturity in the year following their birth. In years when there are too many jackals in an area, however, the young pups do not breed until they are two years old.

▼ *This Golden jackal lives on the grassy plains of the Serengeti National Park in Africa. The jackal is increasing its range and has been seen in Italy.*

KEY FACTS

● **Name**
Golden jackal
(*Canis aureus*)

● **Range**
Widely distributed in East and North Africa, southeast Europe, south Asia to Thailand

● **Habitat**
Usually in open grasslands and scrub; also found near human habitation

● **Appearance**
4 ft (1.3 m) long excluding tail; pale golden brown fur, or yellow with darker brown tips; relatively short hair; a long, black-tipped tail

● **Food**
Omnivorous: seeds, fruit, insects, beetles, lizards, birds, and particularly small rodents; also eats dead animals and hunts the young of small antelopes

● **Breeding**
Usually form stable pairs; groups of up to 20 animals are found if food is plentiful; otherwise they form smaller groups, with one-year-olds helping to raise the pups

● **Status**
Common

Jaguar

The jaguar is a large, powerful South American cat. It belongs to a group of animals known as the "big cats," along with its cousins the lions, tigers, and leopards, and it is the largest cat found in South America. Along with the Snow leopard of central Asia, the jaguar differs from other big cats in that it "coughs" rather than roars, communicating with grunts, snarls, and growls, as well as mewing cries during the mating season.

Stalking the forests

The jaguar is a carnivore (meat eater) and an efficient hunter. Like most other big cats, it cannot run at high speeds for very long in pursuit of its prey, and uses its

▲ *The jaguar is often confused with the leopard: the jaguar (above) is more solidly built, with a large head, short (but strong) limbs, and huge paws. The leopard also has smaller, boxy spots, while the jaguar has large, rosette-like markings.*

strength and short bursts of speed to catch its victims. It also relies heavily on its stealth and the ability to creep up on unsuspecting animals. It then uses the element of surprise to startle and catch them. For this reason, the jaguar prefers to hunt by night under thick cover. It may inhabit open ground if necessary, but can most often be found padding silently through swampland and dense jungle. Indeed, although it mainly hunts on the

KEY FACTS

- **Name**
  Jaguar
  (*Panthera onca*)

- **Range**
  Central and South America, from southern U.S. to central Patagonia

- **Habitat**
  Tropical forests, swamps, savannah

- **Appearance**
  A large, heavily built cat with short, sturdy legs; males may grow up to 8 ft (2.5 m) from head to tail; the fur is yellowish- or reddish-brown with large rosette-shaped markings and pale underparts (although all-black animals are common)

- **Food**
  Some large mammals, small rodents, birds, amphibians, fish

- **Breeding**
  2-4 cubs are born blind, 3 months after mating; the mother rears them alone, suckling them for 6 months; cubs can mate at 3 years

- **Status**
  Endangered

ground, the jaguar has sharp claws and powerful limbs and can climb trees well.

The jaguar preys on a wide variety of animals, including some large mammals such as tapirs, monkeys, and deer; small rodents, birds, fish, reptiles; and amphibians such as frogs and turtles. The jaguar spends much time near water and is an excellent swimmer.

Defending their patch

Jaguars are generally solitary animals, preferring to hunt alone rather than in pairs or large groups. They are also very territorial and defend their territories fiercely, marking the boundaries with strong-smelling urine. Some animals have even been known to escort humans out of their territories, following them from a safe distance in the jungle without attacking and then disappearing just as suddenly as they appeared!

The size of a jaguar's territory depends on the availability of food in the area and ranges from 2-200 sq miles (5-500 km^2). Occasionally, jaguars undertake long journeys, traveling as far as 500 miles (800 km) at once. Scientists are not yet sure of the reason for this.

During the mating season (which is in spring in the northern parts of the jaguar's range), mating pairs meet up together. Just over three months later, the female gives birth to a litter of two to four young in a specially hidden den in the vegetation and rocks. The cubs weigh a mere 25-30 oz (700-850 g) each and are blind at birth, although they are able to see at about 13 days old. The father is absent while they are growing up, having left

their mother immediately after mating. The female rears them alone, suckling them for three to four months and taking them on hunting trips once they reach the age of six months. She is very protective of them and can be extremely aggressive toward intruders — even their own father! The cubs stay with her until they are two years old, at which age they leave to become independent.

A rare sight

Jaguars have been widely hunted for sport as well as for their beautiful skins, and much of their habitat has been destroyed by humans. Today, all eight subspecies of jaguar are seriously endangered.

▲ *This jaguar is "fishing" for its dinner: it crouches, still and silent by the edge of the water, then flips the fish out onto the rocks with its forepaw.*

NATURAL HABITAT

Jaguar

See also **Cheetah, Leopard, Lion, Tiger**

Jellyfish

Jellyfish can be found in every ocean of the world, from the warm tropical seas to the icy polar regions. Most species live near the surface and have bowl-shaped bodies that measure from under an inch to a foot (2-30 cm) in diameter. Beneath their bodies hang long arms and tentacles. Although their bodies are usually colorless, their internal organs can be any color from orange to violet.

Here's the sting

Despite their defenseless and delicate appearance, most of the 250 species of jellyfish are active predators and they can catch and kill large prey such as fish. Even those species that feed on animals so small they can only be seen under a microscope have hidden weapons and are able to protect themselves against the largest predators in the sea. Their dangling tentacles carry poisons to stun their prey. The poison used by some species of jellyfish is very dangerous even to

humans. The Australian Sea Wasp, *Chironex fleckeri,* can cause death in humans within minutes. The sting of a Portuguese man-of-war may cause nausea and shock as well as a burning feeling or numbness.

Because jellyfish do not appear to move much they are often thought of as being inactive, but if the tentacles and arms that hang lazily from the body are magnified, the true nature of the jellyfish is revealed.

▲ *Contrary to popular belief, the Portuguese man-of-war is not a jellyfish. It is a large, deadly, poisonous hydroid that has tentacles as long as 45 ft (14 m) hanging below its floating body.*

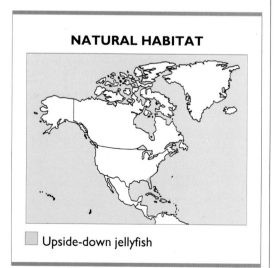

NATURAL HABITAT

Upside-down jellyfish

In some species the tentacles are short and form a frill around the edge of their bodies. These tentacles beat rapidly, forcing water and tiny animals toward the jellyfish's sticky arms. Once the food has stuck to them, it is carried to the mouth and scraped off.

Not all jellyfish feed this way. The North Atlantic giant violet jellyfish (*Cyanea capillata*), which can grow up to 6 ft 9 in (2 m) in diameter, also has extremely long tentacles – up to 117 ft (33.7 m) long. These tentacles spread out like a vast spider's web beneath it. Any small animals that brush against them are instantly harpooned by hundreds of barbed and poisonous darts. At the same time, the tentacle coils up to bring the food up to the mouth where it is swallowed.

Versatile feeders

Another way of gathering food can be seen in the Upside-down jellyfish. These jellyfish have given up floating and have settled on the seabed in the shallow waters around Florida and the West Indies. Here they have flipped themselves upside down so that their frilly arms can move freely in the water. They feed in the same way as the Common jellyfish, picking tiny particles out of the water. However, they can also get energy from sunlight: algae in their arms convert it into food the same way as plants do.

Multiplying numbers

Jellyfish have a complicated life cycle compared to most animals. Adult jellyfish are either male or female and produce either sperm or eggs. The sperm float in the water until taken in by the female. Jellyfish often gather together in vast numbers at certain times of the year to increase the chance of fertilization. Once the sperm has fertilized the eggs, the female releases them into the water and leaves them to float away. In the Common jellyfish they stick to one of its arms and remain there until they hatch.

The larva looks completely different from the adult. It is flat with small tentacles around the edge of its body that it uses like little oars, pushing itself through the water. After a few days of swimming freely the larva starts to sink. As it touches the seabed, a stalk begins to grow from underneath the larva's body. This will soon attach it firmly to the sea bed. After a while, the short tentacles that were used for swimming grow longer and are soon capable of catching food.

As the larva gets bigger it splits its top half from its bottom half. The bottom half then continues to split in half. After about a week there is a stack of developing jellyfish. Once these young jellyfish are self-sufficient, they break off from the stack and float off to grow into adults.

◀ *The bluish arms of the Upside-down jellyfish contain small, plant-like organisms that can supply all the food the jellyfish needs. The algae take energy from sunlight by a process called photosynthesis.*

See also **Hydra**

Kangaroo

Everyone knows that kangaroos, members of the marsupial group of mammals, live in Australia. What many do not know is that kangaroos, and the closely related wallabies, come in all shapes and sizes. The tree kangaroos look like large squirrels with long tails, small ears, and squirrel-like faces. Another group of less well-known kangaroos are the rat kangaroos in the *Potaridae* family. Living up to their name, the nine species in this family look very much like rats and mice.

A typical roo

Of the 45 species of kangaroo, the best known is the Red kangaroo, one of 37 species of large-footed kangaroos whose family name, *Macropodidae*, is extremely descriptive (in Greek, *macro* means large and *pod* means foot). The Red kangaroo has large, flat feet, strong legs, and a long muscular tail to balance itself as it hops

along. The front legs are small and used while feeding but not while the animal hops at high speed, and the arms are relatively short. They are mainly nocturnal animals, with large ears to help them hear better at night.

Along with the big feet and tail, the Red kangaroo is best known for its pouch. Most mammals the size of the Red kangaroo have a pregnancy that lasts around 6 months. Red kangaroos have extremely short gestation times – the young develop in the womb for only 33 days. When a baby kangaroo is born it is

▲ *Male kangaroos "box" with each other to gain access to females, balancing themselves with their muscular tails. The Red kangaroo (shown above) is the largest of all the kangaroos, weighing up to 200 lb (90 kg) – so don't volunteer to enter a boxing contest with one!*

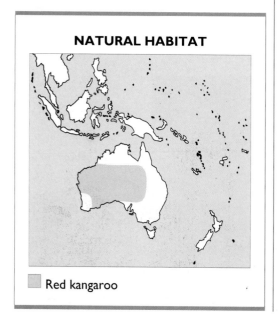

NATURAL HABITAT

Red kangaroo

● **Name**
Red Kangaroo
(*Macropus rufus*)

● **Range**
Much of central and
western Australia,
with highest
concentrations in
the southeast

● **Habitat**
Grasslands,
semideserts

● **Appearance**
Males up to 6½ ft
(2 m) tall (body and
head); a reddish-
brown coat with gray
underbelly; large flat
feet, a long, fat,
muscular tail; the
forelimbs are small
and delicate; a long
face and large ears

● **Food**
Mainly grass, but Red
kangaroos will also
eat the leaves of
small shrubs; they
rarely eat the leaves
of large bushes

● **Breeding**
A single male may
have a harem of
several females;
gestation takes only
33 days, but the
young remains in
the pouch for 9
months following
birth

● **Status**
Common

tiny, blind, hairless, and only about an inch (2.5 cm) long. The only parts of the body that are well developed are the arms, which the baby uses to crawl up the mother's belly into the pouch. The mother does not help the young get to the pouch in any way.

Once in the pouch, the baby attaches itself to one of the mother's teats and spends almost 9 months growing in the pouch. In a way, this "pouch time" is like a second gestation. While in the pouch, the baby kangaroo is known as a joey.

Extra numbers

Life is not easy for a Red kangaroo. Extreme variation in rainfall means that young in the pouch, or even year-old animals that live out of the pouch, often starve to death. However, because of her reproductive system, the Red kangaroo always has another baby ready to replace any that are lost. At any time, a female may have three young at different stages of development: a joey in the pouch, an older yearling outside the pouch, and a fertilized egg waiting for the pouch to become free.

As soon as a baby is born and crawls into the pouch, the female mates and an egg is fertilized. But instead of developing normally, the egg stops growing and waits in the mother's womb. If the joey dies or leaves the pouch, the egg begins developing and about a month later another baby is born.

▼ *Kangaroos are well known for the way they hop across the grasslands. This mother probably has a second baby in her pouch. While the baby feeds on a rich, creamy milk, a second teat provides watery food for the older offspring.*

Kangaroo rat

KEY FACTS

● **Name**
Merriam's
kangaroo rat
(*Dipodomys merriami*)

● **Range**
Southwestern North
America

● **Habitat**
Deserts

● **Appearance**
Head and body
length of 6 in
(16 cm); pale brown
upperparts and white
beneath with a white
stripe running over
the back; a large
head and large eyes;
short forepaws; long
hind legs; a long tail
measuring 5-6 in
(13-16 cm), ending in
a tuft of fur; some
individuals may weigh
up to 5 oz (150 g)

● **Food**
Seeds, leaves, fruit,
plant stems

● **Breeding**
Females bear up to
3 litters of 1-3 young
per year, usually
about 4 weeks after
mating; the young
remain in the burrow
for 6 weeks

● **Status**
Widespread

The kangaroo rat (not to be confused with the rat kangaroo) is a small creature with long hind legs and tail and a habit of hopping erratically from place to place. It is because the kangaroo rat shares these features with the kangaroo of Australia that it was given its common name. Similar features are also found in the jerboa and the kangaroo mouse, which, like the kangaroo rat, inhabit dry places.

Kangaroo rats are rodents and belong to the same family as pocket mice and kangaroo mice. There are some 24 species of kangaroo rat, all of which are found in western and southern North America.

The kangaroo rat lives in dry or semidry regions. It favors open country with little vegetation where it can move about easily, and sandy soil that is easy to dig. During

▲ *Like this Merriam's kangaroo rat, most species have coloring that is pale brown above and white underneath. Some may have a white stripe on each hip and a furry tuft at the end of their tails.*

the day it hides in its burrow beneath the ground and does not emerge until it is completely dark. Unlike many other animals that are active at night, the kangaroo rat shuns all kind of light, remaining in its burrow even when there is bright moonlight. It will also stay beneath ground if it is very wet.

Surviving the heat

The kangaroo rat is well adapted to its hot dry habitat. It can survive for long periods without drinking because its body processes are able to extract water from food, especially from succulent plants. However, it does obtain some water from drinking dew. By resting up during the day, the kangaroo rat avoids high temperatures. If it does get overheated, it can lower its body temperature by producing large amounts of saliva and licking its entire body. As the saliva evaporates in the heat, the body cools down. The kangaroo rat also takes frequent dust baths. These free the fur of foreign particles, which prevents it from getting matted and stops sores from developing on the skin.

Processing their food

Kangaroo rats feed on a wide variety of plants and eat almost every part – seeds, stems, leaves, and fruit. They will also eat insects occasionally. They hoard away some of the food they find in food stores placed near their nests, ready to use when food and water is scarce.

The kangaroo rat transports its food to the store in special cheek pouches. These are made of folds of skin and are lined with fur. To remove the food in its pouches, the kangaroo rat places its forepaws on its cheeks and squeezes until the food spills out.

Scientists have found evidence that the kangaroo rats process at least some of their food before storing it. They place it in shallow hollows in the sand and leave it there until it has dried out. This helps to preserve the food so that it doesn't get moldy. Then they transport it to more permanent food stores.

Owls and rattlesnakes prey on the kangaroo rat. Its main defense against

these predators is its highly developed hearing. Scientists have shown that kangaroo rats can pick up the faintest rustling sounds from a considerable distance, even the soft swish of a bird's wings or the movement of a snake's body over the earth.

A good listener

Such sensitive hearing is made possible by a special mechanism in which dome-shaped bones lie over the middle ears, making noises sound louder. Devices such as these are very important to animals living in deserts, where it is vital to be able to detect predators from a distance. In addition, it is thought that these special organs may help the kangaroo rat to balance while sitting up and leaping about.

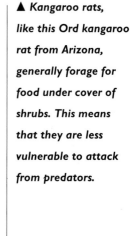

▲ *Kangaroo rats, like this Ord kangaroo rat from Arizona, generally forage for food under cover of shrubs. This means that they are less vulnerable to attack from predators.*

NATURAL HABITAT

Merriam's kangaroo rat

Kelp and other seaweeds

If you take a trip to the seaside, you will almost certainly see masses of brown, green, or red matter floating on the surface of the water or attached to rocks and piers. These growths are called seaweed, which is a type of multicellular marine alga.

Seaweed colors

Seaweeds occur in three forms: brown (*Phaeophyta*), green (*Chlorophyta*), and red algae (*Rhodophyta*). The color of a seaweed is determined by substances called

NATURAL HABITAT

Giant kelp

▲ *Several types of brown algae are known as kelp. These kelps (Laminaria digitata) are clinging to the surface of a rock using structures called hold-fasts. The hold-fast produces an extremely strong glue, which fixes the seaweed to the solid foundation. Although the hold-fast looks like a root, no food is extracted through it: it is simply an anchor. Species from the genus* **Laminaria** *are particularly abundant along coasts of North America and Europe.*

pigments, which absorb light from the sun and use the energy to produce food in a process called photosynthesis. Plants contain a green pigment called chlorophyll, but, in addition to chlorophyll, seaweed contains pigments with different colors.

Brown algae are some of the most highly evolved seaweeds and include many larger species of seaweed and the kelps. Kelps are the largest seaweeds and can grow in forests hundreds of feet high, with many smaller seaweeds growing on their stems.

Seaweeds are best described as plants. However, recent classifications separate single-celled algae into the protist kingdom. Other protists include animal-like organisms such as the amoeba and fungus-like organisms such as slime molds.

Shapes and sizes

In clear, tropical waters, seaweeds can grow to depths of up to 660 ft (200 m). In colder, murkier water they will not grow as deep. There are about 8000 species of seaweed, and those that float far out to sea often look quite unlike those that are found on the coast.

Despite many differences, most seaweeds are made up of three sections: the hold-fast, the branching blade, and the stem-like stipe. The hold-fast produces a powerful glue that fixes the seaweed to a solid foundation. The blade is a large, sheet-like area through which the seaweed absorbs sunlight. It uses the energy obtained in this way to feed and grow.

KEY FACTS

● **Name**
Giant kelp
(*Macrocystis pyrifera*)

● **Range**
Water surrounding
North and South
America, South Africa,
Australia, New
Zealand, and the
islands near Antarctica

● **Habitat**
Shallow water

● **Appearance**
Brown seaweed; large
hold-fast clings to the
ocean floor; hollow,
stem-like stipe, with
long, branching blades
on which there are
hollow gas bladders;
blades grow to 330 ft
(100 m) in length;
growth rate up to
17½ in (45 cm) a day
recorded

● **Life cycle**
Reproduces in two
alternating phases – a
spore-producing and
a sexually reproducing
phase; reproduction
occurs only at
temperatures lower
than 64-68°F
(18-20°C)

● **Uses**
Used to make algin
for ice cream and
tires; fertilizer

● **Status**
Common and
widespread

Organic material is transported from the blade to the hold-fast through the stem-like stipe.

Some species such as *Sargassum* seaweeds form large, free-floating meadows in tropical seas and have no hold-fast. They are particularly abundant off the coast of the West Indies. It is from here that they derive their everyday name, gulfweed. In the Caribbean, an area of the Atlantic Ocean is so thickly strewn with gulfweed that it is called the Sargasso Sea.

Seaweed for supper

Seaweed has a high mineral and vitamin content, and several species – notably dulse (*Palmaria palmata*), laver (*Porphyra* spp.), and sea lettuce (*Ulva* spp.) – are popular in soups and stews. In many coastal areas, seaweeds are also used as livestock feed and fertilizers, particularly in colder climates, on small, mountainous islands, and where the terrain makes the land difficult to cultivate.

Iodine

Brown seaweeds such as kelps were once an important source of iodine. Iodine is used in medicine as an antiseptic (bacteria-killing) cleaner and to treat goiter (swollen thyroid glands in the neck).

Reproduction

Most seaweeds have two growing phases: a spore-producing phase and a sexually reproducing phase. The phases alternate so that the spores develop into a seaweed that bears sex organs. The sex organs produce male and female reproductive cells, which join together and develop into a spore-producing seaweed.

Flotation bladders

The largest known seaweed is the Giant kelp (*Macrocystis pyrifera*). It has a large hold-fast, a hollow stipe, a long branching stalk, and 330-ft- (100-m-) long blades on which there are hollow gas bladders. The gas bladders help the blades stay afloat.

◄ *Giant kelp (Macrocystis pyrifera) is a mineral-rich seaweed. It also produces algin, which is used as a dietary supplement and taken orally in the form of kelp pills. Algin is also used to make tires, and it is added to ice cream before freezing to prevent it from forming ice crystals.*

See also **Alga, Amoeba, Ocean**

Kestrel

Kestrels are among the most highly specialized birds of prey. Their long narrow wings are made for lengthy, swift flight. Strong beaks and equally strong feet with sharp talons are ideally suited to a hunting lifestyle and also play a part in defense, particularly among the young.

Kestrels are the smallest and the most common birds belonging to the falcon group. They are found on all of the world's continents with the exception of Antarctica. In North America the species

▲ *Sometimes, instead of hovering in midair, the kestrel will hunt from a convenient post. Unlike other falcons, it rarely catches prey on the wing, but it has been seen to steal another bird's catch while in flight.*

are represented by the American kestrel, which is also popularly known as the Sparrow hawk (not to be confused with the European sparrowhawk *Accipiter nisus*, which is a separate species). In Europe and Africa the main species is the Common kestrel. Both the Common and the American kestrels are very similar in habits and appearance.

Country or city dweller?
The kestrel usually inhabits open or fairly open countryside, often near woodlands. However, in some places it also takes up residence in cities, where it has shown a remarkable ability to adapt to the urban environment. It is perhaps best known for its habit of hovering, and for this reason is sometimes known as the windhover.

The kestrel hovers in midair up to 100 ft (about 30 m) above the ground, using its remarkably keen eyesight to watch for the movements of small creatures on the earth below. It hunts over open spaces

NATURAL HABITAT

American kestrel

▲ *This kestrel has spotted its prey (probably a small rodent) in the grass and has dropped to the ground to seize it in its long, sharp talons.*

such as unused land, the side of the highway, a field, or a grassy plain. In such places it may hover for an hour, fixing its eyes on the ground and watching for any movement indicating the presence of a small creature. Every now and again the bird will drop to the ground to capture its prey. The main items in the kestrel's diet are small mammals such as rodents, small birds, earthworms, and large insects such as grasshoppers and moths.

Acrobatic displays

Kestrels normally begin their courtship in the spring – usually late March or early April. They do not build nests themselves; instead they often take over the abandoned nests of other fairly large birds such as crows, buzzards, and magpies. Kestrels also nest in hollow trees, on cliff ledges and, in cities, in crevices and on ledges on tall buildings.

The courtship display of the male kestrel consists of a series of aerial acrobatics with which he tries to attract the attention of the female and draw her to the nesting site. He flies around in circles above the perched female, taking three or four wing beats and following these with a glide. This flight is interspersed with dives. Throughout the display he utters the characteristic cry "kee-kee-kee." Sometimes the female will fly up from her perch to join him, while the male continues flying around and above her.

Four to six eggs are laid and are kept warm – usually by the female, although sometimes by the male, who also feeds the female. The chicks hatch in about four weeks and grow feathers four weeks later.

KEY FACTS

● **Name**
American kestrel or Sparrow hawk (*Falco sparverius*)

● **Range**
Most of North and South America except the tundra; birds in Canada and mountainous areas may migrate south for the winter

● **Habitat**
Open countryside, cities

● **Appearance**
9-11 in (23-28 cm) from head to tail; adults have rusty backs barred with black and rusty tails with black bars at the tip; dark blue inner wings; the head has patches of white, black, and rust

● **Food**
Rodents, small birds, insects; occasionally carrion, meat, and bread scraps from bird feeders

● **Breeding**
4-6 eggs, buff-brown thickly speckled with dark reddish-brown; the eggs hatch after 4 weeks and the young birds fledge 4 weeks after that

● **Status**
Widespread

Killdeer

KEY FACTS

● **Name**
Killdeer
(*Charadrius vociferus*)

● **Range**
North America,
the Caribbean, and
coastal western
South America

● **Habitat**
Fields, airports,
riverbanks, shores

● **Appearance**
9-11 in (23-28 cm);
a white front, with
2 distinctive black
breastbands; a dark
gray-brown head and
back; a long, rounded
tail, with a black band
and a white tip; a
slim black bill

● **Food**
Mainly insects

● **Breeding**
Aerial courtship
flights; nest in the
open, in pastures,
meadows, and gravel
beds; nest is a hollow
in the ground lined
with pebbles or
grasses; the eggs are
laid March-July,
usually 4; both
parents incubate
them for 24 days

● **Status**
Common

Throughout North America, in those areas that are not covered in snow, and as far south as Peru and Chile, the plaintive "killdee, killdee" of the killdeer can be heard along seashore, lakes, and rivers. Of course it is this call that gives the killdeer its name; and it is such a sad, distressing sound that many people, when they hear it for the first time, think that it must be the cry of a young bird or a bird in pain.

The killdeer is probably the most widely distributed and best known of all North American wading birds. However, although it is well adapted for life along the water's edge, the killdeer (unlike most shorebirds) is often found many miles from water, in open fields and grasslands.

▲ *From western North America, down to Argentina, the killdeer is a common sight near lakes, rivers, and shores. Its long legs enable it to wade through shallow waters in search of food, but it is also at home in drier grassland habitats.*

Family likeness

The killdeer is a type of plover. It is a small, noisy bird, with a neat, tapering body and pert, round head. Its most distinctive marking, if you are trying to distinguish between several similar grassland and marshland birds, is a double ring of black feathers across the upper part of its breast – one of these bands extends right around the killdeer's neck.

When on the ground it moves like other plovers, running in short bursts at quite a speed. It struts around the grassland, probing the ground with its strong, straight bill, looking for insects and grubs. It can also be seen along shorelines and riverbanks, dipping its bill into the muddy banks in search of aquatic insects. It often follows plows in its hunt for a tasty meal, searching for worms and larvae that have been exposed. When it takes to the air its flight is swift but erratic; it flies low and skims the ground.

Breeding patterns

Spring is the mating season, and killdeers perform a ritual mating display. They hover high above the ground and circle over a suitable nesting site. The nest is simply a shallow dip in the ground lined with fine twigs and grasses.

Killdeers are caring parents who protect their eggs and young by flying into the

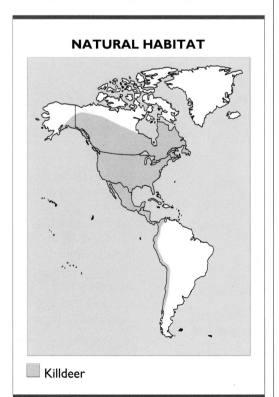

NATURAL HABITAT

Killdeer

▲ *The killdeer lays its eggs in a hollow in the ground. The parents are surprisingly well-camouflaged against the rocky scrublands. Even if the parents leave the nest for a short time, the eggs are relatively safe because they, too, are well camouflaged by their buff color with dark spots.*

faces of intruding animals or people. They are also skilled actors who perform what is referred to as the "broken wing act." This involves pretending that one of their wings is broken and running away from the nest, calling piteously and dragging one wing and their tail along the ground. This draws predators away from the nesting site, protecting the young birds.

For the first 10 days after hatching, however, the young killdeers are open to attack and many die before reaching adulthood. It is about three weeks before they are able to fly.

Killdeers are seldom seen in large flocks: they tend to forage on their own, or in pairs during the breeding season. Occasionally, however, groups of up to 50 have been seen patrolling the grasslands and making their characteristic short flights. They are extremely noisy birds, which gives them their Latin name, *Charadrius vociferus.*

Kingfisher

Many of us think of kingfishers as small, brightly colored birds that are seen at the edges of ponds or rivers, darting into the shallow water to catch fish, their favorite food. However, the Kingfisher family contains 95 different species of birds that are found throughout the world in a variety of habitats and feed on a wide range of food.

The Kingfisher family is split into two subfamilies: the forest kingfishers (*Daceloninae*) and the fish-eating kingfishers (*Alcedininae*). Only three species are found

▲ *This brightly colored Common kingfisher* (**Alcedo atthis**) *is flying back to its nest in a riverbank, with a fish gripped tightly in its beak.*

in North America: the Green kingfisher and the Ringed kingfisher, which are South and Central American species that can be found in some southern states, and the Belted kingfisher, which is found throughout North America.

King of the fishers

The fish-eating kingfishers are fairly small, squat birds with large heads and short tails. They have long, sharp-pointed beaks, sometimes colored red or yellow, which are extremely strong and well adapted to catching fish. Many of them, such as the Common kingfisher of Eurasia and northern Africa, have bright, distinctive feathers (often greens and blues), and some have large, upward-standing crests on top of their heads. Their legs, which are only used for perching, are very short, and they have unusual feet with three toes pointing forward and one backward. They can fly fast and straight, but not very far.

These birds are skilled fishers. They have regular perches – usually a branch overhanging a river or pond, or a stake on a pier along the coast – where they sit, upright and motionless, watching for their prey. Once they have spotted a fish, they dive headlong into the water, seizing it in their tough beaks. They have to aim well as they do this, because they close their eyes under water.

Some species do not use a perch, but hover above the water until they spot their prey. These kingfishers will also catch and eat large tadpoles, crabs,

KEY FACTS

● **Name**
Belted kingfisher (*Ceryle alcyon*)

● **Range**
Alaska and Canada, down to southern U.S.; winters in northern South America and the Galapagos Islands

● **Habitat**
Usually near water; streams, lakes, bays, coasts

● **Appearance**
Medium-sized bird, measuring 13 in (33 cm) from head to tail, with a large head and bill; blue-gray above and white below with a bushy crest and a broad gray breast band; females also have a rusty breastband

● **Food**
Mainly fish; also large tadpoles, insects, crustaceans, young birds, small mammals

● **Breeding**
5-8 white eggs are laid from April to July and are incubated for 23-24 days

● **Status**
Widespread

▲ *When it has caught a fish, the kingfisher flies back to its perch, where it beats the fish against the wood to kill it. Then the bird swallows it whole, tossing it in the air so that it is swallowed headfirst. Any food that the kingfisher cannot digest is brought up again in small pellets. This picture is of a male Belted kingfisher (Ceryle alcyon) – the female is similar but has a band of rust-colored feathers across her chest.*

crayfish, insects, young birds, and even small mammals. As well as looking out for food, the kingfisher must be aware of any predators in the area, such as falcons or hawks. If they are attacked by these large birds of prey, they will often dive below the surface of the water to escape.

The forest kingfishers are perhaps less familiar to most people than their cousins. They are generally larger in size than the fish-eating species and their bills are often wider and flatter. Many of them live far from water, in dry savannahs or forests, and they feed on large insects and small reptiles, birds, amphibians, and mammals. The largest species is the Australian Kookaburra or Laughing Jackass, so called because of its strange "laughing" cries that can be heard at dawn and dusk.

Kingfishers are solitary birds, spending their time alone in small feeding territories except during the breeding season in the spring and summer. Then males and females meet together to defend larger territories that contain their nesting and feeding areas.

Nesting in the riverbanks

The fishing species dig their burrows in riverbanks, using their bills to dig and pushing out the dirt with their feet. These are usually tunnels 3-7 ft (1-2 m) long, extending horizontally and ending in a large, unlined chamber. The forest kingfishers also nest in holes, although some species such as the Kookaburra prefer hollow trees, and some tropical species use abandoned termite nests.

Many species of kingfisher have two broods of young per year, but the Belted kingfisher only lays one clutch of six or seven white eggs. These are incubated by both parents for 23-24 days. The young are naked, blind, and totally defenseless when they hatch. They stay in the nest for three or four weeks, during which time they are fed on fish and crustaceans by the male and female.

NATURAL HABITAT

Belted kingfisher

Kiwi

The kiwi is famous as the national bird of New Zealand. It is a flightless bird, because on the islands where it lives there were no large mammals to attack it and it simply did not need to use its wings. Kiwis are shy, retiring birds, so it is unusual to see them in the wild. They are becoming rarer as humans and mammals invade their territory. There are three species, all very similar, living in different parts of New Zealand.

Feathered shape

While most birds have different types of feathers on different parts of their body (long tail and wing feathers and shorter feathers on the head and breast), kiwis are covered with feathers of an even length and similar texture. They look like round, brown furry mammals with long noses, more like anteaters than birds. The feathers are predominantly dark brown, but in some species they are streaked and mottled with a paler shade.

They do have wings, which are about 2 in (5 cm) long, but they can hardly move them. There are bare patches beneath the wings, and when it sleeps, the kiwi tucks its head under its wing. Their legs are stout and strong, and spaced quite

KEY FACTS

● **Name**
Common or
Brown kiwi
(*Apteryx australis*)

● **Range**
South Island
and Stewart Island,
New Zealand

● **Habitat**
Forests

● **Appearance**
20 in (50 cm); a
round, brown bird
with a long beak;
stout gray legs

● **Food**
Carnivorous; mainly
worms, insects,
centipedes

● **Breeding**
One or two large
white eggs laid in a
burrow dug by the
male; incubated by
the male

● **Status**
Widespread within a
limited range

◄ *Looking more like a hairy mammal with lizard-like feet than a feathered bird, the Brown kiwi is well disguised in the forests of New Zealand.*

widely apart, so that as it walks or runs it rolls from side to side.

Foraging for food

The kiwi has a much keener sense of smell than most other birds: its nostrils are at the tip of its beak so it can sniff out the grubs and worms that are its favorite food. The kiwi only comes out to forage at night – another reason why so few are seen in the wild.

The whole time they forage, pairs of kiwis call to each other with a distinctive, loud, sometimes rasping call so that they can stay together and keep control of their territory. The breeding season is long: eggs may be laid anytime from late winter to late summer. The male takes a couple of months to prepare the nest – a burrow in the ground. The female lays a single egg or occasionally two. Like most other flightless birds, the male usually takes charge of the incubation of the egg, which is large (as much as a quarter of the weight of the female). The eggs have very

rich, large yolks, and the incubation period is very long – the eggs do not hatch until about 12 weeks after they have been laid. By this time, the young birds have already developed their feathers inside the egg. The food provided by the yolk keeps them going until they are old enough to forage for themselves.

The introduction of predatory mammals such as stoats, weasels, cats, and dogs has drastically reduced the number of kiwis. Also in some places their habitat is being restricted by modern development. Teams of people try to catch and move the kiwis before their habitat is destroyed, and many have been moved to New Zealand's animal reserves. One species, the Little spotted kiwi, became extinct in its original range, but before it died out, it was captured and later released to roam wild on a small island, where it has thrived.

▲ *Because they cannot fly, and because there are few predators to attack their young, kiwis build their nests at ground level. This kiwi is looking after its young in a burrow beneath a log. The young kiwis already have their feathers when they hatch and are soon able to go out to hunt for food themselves.*

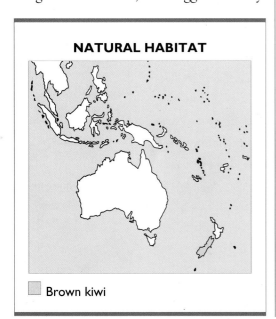

NATURAL HABITAT

Brown kiwi

Koala

Koalas, sometimes called koala bears, are not even distantly related to the bear family. Like every native mammal of Australia, the koala is a marsupial, or pouched mammal, and newborn koalas spend the first weeks of their lives in the pouch. Physically, koalas are also very different from bears. They are much smaller – they only weigh 15-18 lb (7-9 kg) – and have small bodies and relatively large arms.

Special food

Some animals are not choosy about what they eat: the African elephant eats almost

▲ *The young koala, once it has emerged from the pouch, spends much time on its mother's back. She forages for tender eucalyptus shoots.*

any plant material; and the Red fox eats anything it can find, even taking food from garbage cans. Scientists call those animals generalists. Other animals, called diet specialists, will only eat certain foods. These animals include species such as the Giant panda, which eats only bamboo, and the koala, whose taste for leaves extends only to eucalyptus trees.

Specialist feeders frequently eat things that other animals do not like or cannot digest. The panda's bamboo diet is very rough and difficult to eat, leaving most of the bamboo for the pandas who like the challenge! For most animals, the strong flavor and bitterness of eucalyptus prevents them from eating the leaves of these trees. You might have come across the penetrating scent and flavor of eucalyptus in cold remedies and cough drops. The koala, however, has developed a taste for these leaves and is able to specialize in eucalyptus.

The koala is adapted to eating eucalyptus in several different ways. To begin with, it releases a special chemical from its liver, which helps digest the leaves. In addition, it has special bacteria in its digestive system that break down the chemicals found in eucalyptus leaves. A diet of leaves, and nothing but leaves, is also very hard on the teeth; leaves are full of a chemical called silica, the same substance that sand is made from. To avoid wearing out its teeth, the koala has broad, flat, hardwearing back teeth, or molars, that easily crush and process the leaves it eats.

KEY FACTS

- **Name**
  Koala (*Phascolarctos cinereus*)

- **Range**
  Southeastern Australia

- **Habitat**
  Eucalyptus forests below an altitude of 2000 ft (600 m)

- **Appearance**
  Gray to reddish-gray coat, white belly and ear fringes; large black claws and a large rectangular nose; adults weigh 11-18 lb (5-8 kg), with males being about 20 percent larger than females

- **Food**
  Very specific in its diet, eats only the leaves of trees in the Genus *Eucalyptus*

- **Breeding**
  A single young weighing 1 lb (0.5 kg) is born after a gestation of 35 days; the young spends many months in the pouch and is only weaned at 5 months

- **Status**
  Common within a small range

Family life

Most koalas live alone, although occasionally they form small groups of two females and their young. Both males and females hold territories, with the male having a larger territory that covers the territories of several females and, perhaps, one or more nonbreeding males. Breeding takes place in the spring (November in the southern hemisphere). Males mate with several females, but females usually mate with only a single male. After a short gestation (pregnancy) of 35 days, a small baby is born, weighing a pound or so (0.5 kg). Like its relatives, kangaroos, the baby then spends several months in the mother's pouch, where it is safe and near its food supply – mother's milk.

Perhaps the greatest misunderstanding over koalas concerns their behavior. Although they are small and fluffy, they can hardly be described as sweet and cuddly. Koalas, in fact, have a reputation for being unsociable and rather nasty, using their sharp claws not only to climb

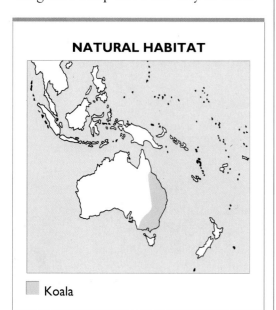

NATURAL HABITAT

☐ Koala

trees, but also to fend off predators and fight off intruders in the breeding season. They are slow-moving creatures, eating and sleeping most of the time.

Koalas are common where there is the right food and environment. Obviously, their great dependence on eucalyptus forests means that they can only exist in areas with this particular type of tree. In some national parks, koalas have become so numerous that many young do not survive because there is not enough food.

To protect these populations, and to expand the area available to koalas, the Australian government has begun a program to move koalas to colonize new eucalyptus forests; they have also been moved to offshore islands where eucalyptus exists, but where koalas never lived because they could not cross the sea.

In the United States, koalas have been introduced to San Diego, on the west coast. Eucalyptus trees brought from Australia provide a habitat for them.

▲ *When the koala leaps from tree to tree, it can grab hold of branches with its clawed paws. Its "thumb" and "forefinger" wrap around one way, while the remaining three fingers wrap around the branch the other way to give a firm grip.*

See also **Eucalyptus**

Komodo dragon

▶ *It is difficult to see how a lizard as large as the Komodo dragon could hide, but it suddenly leaps out of hiding to attack its prey. Adults work together to tear apart carcasses of dead animals such as this goat. Goats were introduced to the islands where the dragons live, and their habit of attacking such domesticated animals made them unpopular with local people. They are now endangered.*

The Komodo dragon is the largest living lizard. It can grow to over 10 ft (3 m) in length and is not only larger, but also bulkier than most lizards. Usually, a lizard's tail represents about two thirds of its length, but with these monsters, the tail is only half its total length. Komodo dragons prowl around the islands where they live on stout legs with long claws, looking like a dinosaur or monster from a science fiction movie.

Komodo dragons are not the only lizards to be compared with dinosaurs. When scientists first discovered fossils of dinosaurs, they thought that they were the fossils of some long-extinct members of the lizard family. They called them dinosaurs, combining two Greek words, meaning fearful lizard. The lizard suborder as a whole is known as *Sauria*.

Great lengths

These giants among lizards are only found on a few islands in the island chain of Indonesia east of Java. They were first found on the island of Komodo at the beginning of the twentieth century. Here there were no big cats or other large carnivores, so Komodo dragons established themselves as the largest and strongest meat eaters. Young dragons eat mainly insects and smaller species of

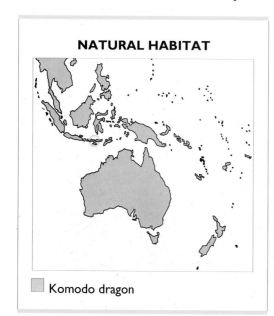

NATURAL HABITAT

▢ Komodo dragon

lizard. As they develop, they find larger and larger prey, going from rats and birds up to pigs and deer when fully grown. As well as hunting for live prey, they feed on the carcasses of dead animals. They are stealthy hunters, lurking in shrubs and bushes, and can move surprisingly fast when they need to on their short legs.

Maneating monsters?

If you came across a Komodo dragon in the wild, it would probably watch you with interest, just as you might watch it. It is unlikely that it would attack you, but if it came upon someone who had collapsed in a state of exhaustion, it would not hestitate to tear the body apart like a carcass. There have been reports of people being bitten by Komodo dragons and dying from their wounds.

Komodo dragons are voracious feeders. Two adult dragons often work together, gripping the meat in their teeth, digging their claws into the ground and jerking their heads backward in order to get at the flesh. If younger dragons threaten them, the adults snap at them and drive them away. Indeed, if adults are hungry,

they seem to have no qualms about eating their young: examination of their feces has proved that they are cannibalistic.

Tongue testing

Like the other monitor lizards, Komodo dragons have long, spindly, forked tongues. They constantly flick their tongues out as though they are tasting the air. This idea is not far from the truth. These lizards use their tongues to draw air into their mouths toward the sensory organs in the roof of the mouth. These sense certain chemicals in the air: the animals are not tasting or smelling the chemicals, but the information is used by the dragon to find water or hunt for food.

Male Komodo dragons often fight for their rights during the breeding season. They rear up on their hind legs, with tails behind to steady themselves, and wrestle with each other until one falls over. The females bury the eggs in the ground and the young fend for themselves.

▼ *Komodo dragons have a lumbering walk, but can move rapidly if they need to. They are also capable of climbing trees or swimming in the sea.*

KEY FACTS

● **Name**
Komodo dragon
(*Varanus komodoensis*)

● **Range**
Komodo; some
Indonesian islands

● **Habitat**
Grasslands

● **Appearance**
Large, leathery
skinned lizards, up
to 10 ft (3 m) long;
almost black in color;
a heavy body, large
clawed feet

● **Food**
Carnivore, eating
anything from insects
to pigs and deer

● **Breeding**
Lays about 15 soft-
shelled eggs that are
buried in the ground;
no parental care

● **Status**
Endangered

Kookaburra

There are five species of Kookaburra, found in Australia, New Guinea, and the surrounding islands. The best known kookaburra is the Laughing kookaburra, one of Australia's commonest birds.

Although it does not often catch fish, it is actually one of the largest kingfishers in the world. Kookaburras are woodland birds and may be seen on the ground,

▲ *This kookaburra is busy bringing up a young family: it has a fat grub gripped firmly in its beak. The beak is similar in shape to that of the kingfisher – a close relative.*

searching for food, or perched on a branch, scanning the area for prey (small reptiles, amphibians and insects).

Laughing call

The most distinctive thing about the Laughing kookaburra is its laugh, which gives it its name. This is one of the commonest sounds of the Australian countryside. It makes a boisterous sound, a chuckle or repeated "kook-kook-kook" developing into a rising, jerkily shouted "kook-kook-kook-ka-ka-ka" which slowly fades. This call, coupled with the kookaburra's large, brilliant, staring eyes, makes it a very strange bird. The call is most often uttered in a serenade at sunrise or sunset and usually warns others of danger, or acts as a deterrent to other birds that are thinking of encroaching on the kookaburra's territory.

These territories may be quite large, anything from one to four acres (0.4-1.6 hectares). The territory is shared by a group of kookaburras, usually a male, his mate, and two or three of their female offspring. They are usually found in eucalyptus forest and woodland, but have spread out to occupy farmland and suburban gardens, as long as there are suitable hollows in the trees for nesting.

Kookaburras are somewhat lazy when it comes to nest building. They often use the same hole year after year, which may be in a tree, a bank, a termite mound, or a suitable hole in a building. They do not line the nest at all, and the whole group

(male, female, and aunts) share the duties of incubating the eggs and feeding the young. When hatched, the babies are helpless. For several months, the young birds are allowed to remain in their parents' territory. However, when the next breeding season approaches the

▲ *Kookaburras are large birds and very common in Australian woodlands. Their well-known call is heard mainly in the morning and the evening.*

young males are driven from the home territory, but the females are allowed to stay and help to rear the next brood.

Feeding habits
Like many birds, the young are fed on a diet of insects and earthworms. As they get older they learn to hunt lizards, frogs, and other small vertebrates. However, kookaburras do not have the sharp, hooked beak or strong talons of other birds of prey such as eagles and hawks. Instead, they grip their prey in their beak and use their strong neck muscles to beat the creature to death. Once a kookaburra has devoured an animal it regurgitates and spits out pellets of indigestible material such as bones and fur.

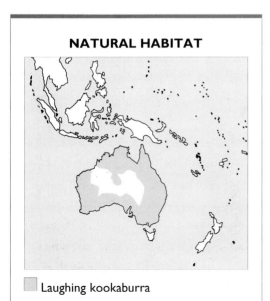

NATURAL HABITAT

Laughing kookaburra

See also **Kingfisher**

Ladybug

▲ *Ladybugs sometimes gather in large numbers to hibernate and are easy to see on plants or on the ground. Their bright colors act as a warning to predators that they don't taste good. If they are injured, a bad-tasting fluid leaks from their leg joints, which deters most ants and birds.*

Ladybug is the popular name for a helpful little insect that should be encouraged to grow in every garden. Although known as bugs, they are in fact beetles. Their brightly colored, usually spotted, hard wing cases cover a pair of delicate wings, which they use to fly to new feeding grounds or to escape from predators. But most of the time they prefer to crawl around those plants that harbor their favorite food supply – aphids.

Feeding machines

There are thousands of species of ladybug: you might think of them as being red with black spots, but some have white spots, some are yellow and black, some have stripes, and some have plain wing cases. They are found in many different habitats, including gardens, farmland, mountains, and desert. Some live in tropical regions, but they are less common there.

Aphids are common garden pests that are often found on plants such as roses, tomatoes, and certain types of bean. Farmers and gardeners used to try to control the aphids (greenfly, whitefly, and blackfly) by spraying their plants with chemicals. Unfortunately, these chemicals killed off the ladybugs as well. However, many pesticides are now banned and ladybugs are making a comeback. In some countries ladybugs are on sale to gardeners to help them control aphids.

When citrus fruit were first grown by farmers in California at the end of the nineteenth century, the trees were

◀ *The larvae look quite different from the adult ladybugs. However, the young are even more popular with gardeners because they eat so many aphids.*

attacked by scale bugs. An Australian ladybug was introduced and saved the citrus fruit groves in the area.

Ladybugs can eat a fantastic number of aphids in their lifetime. It has been estimated that during the 10-15 days when they are growing at their fastest, before reaching adulthood, they can eat up to 50 insects a day. Adults eat up to 30 a day. One ladybug in captivity was seen to eat something like 3000 insects before it reached adulthood.

Changing form

Like other insects, ladybugs go through a larval stage. Females lay their eggs under leaves, close to a supply of aphids. When the eggs hatch, small, black larvae emerge and start their feeding frenzy. They have six legs and a tapered abdomen (the tail section of the body). If there are not enough aphids for them to feed on they will happily eat their brothers and sisters.

Once fully grown, the larva fastens itself to a leaf or stem, often in quite an exposed place, and sheds its skin, revealing a pupa case underneath. After five days, the adult ladybug emerges from the pupa. It is a plain color to start with, but soon develops its pattern.

This whole process takes less than a month, so several families can be raised each year. The adult ladybugs hibernate through the winter, often in quite exposed places. They may gather together and in some parts of southwestern North America they look like a heavy blanket of color on the ground when they hibernate. Occasionally they gather inside outbuildings or even invade houses. The following summer, as soon as the aphids become active again, the adults set to work eating the pests and laying eggs.

Ladybugs are found in most parts of the world; their original range was more limited, but they have spread rapidly.

KEY FACTS

- **Name**
  Ladybug family (*Coccinellidae*), includes Seven spot ladybug (*Coccinella septapunctata*)

- **Range**
  Worldwide, apart from arctic zones; rare in tropics

- **Habitat**
  Woodlands, farmland and gardens

- **Appearance**
  Rounded insects with bright wing cases; black heads and legs; Seven spot ladybug is red with 7 black spots

- **Food**
  Mainly aphids; a few are herbivorous

- **Breeding**
  Eggs are laid on the underside of a leaf; goes through larval and pupal stages; no parental care

- **Status**
  Widespread

See also **Beetle**

Lake, river, and estuary

To you or me, a life out of water is perfectly natural and unstressful. For most creatures, however, dry land is deadly.

About 70 percent of the planet's surface is covered by essential, life-giving water. Most of this is stored in seas and oceans. Less than 3 percent is made up of freshwater, and two-thirds of this is stored as the Arctic and Antarctic ice caps. The remainder occurs mostly as groundwater beneath the earth, which supplies wells and springs. This leaves about 0.014 percent of freshwater in habitats, such as lakes, ponds, rivers, and streams, or in habitats with a mixture of freshwater and salt water, such as estuaries. Most lakes are full of freshwater, but some, such as the Caspian Sea in Eurasia, consist of salt water.

Lakes and ponds

One main feature that distinguishes lakes and ponds from rivers, streams, and estuaries is that lakes and ponds are full of

▲ *Despite being rare, freshwater streams and rivers are a haven for a vast range of animal and plant life.*

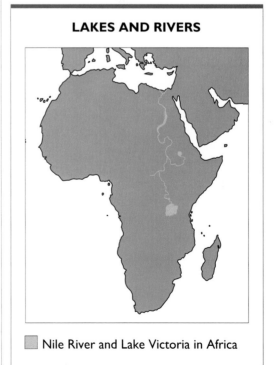

LAKES AND RIVERS

☐ Nile River and Lake Victoria in Africa

still water, which does not cause flowing currents or tides. These quieter waters are particularly suitable for microscopic plankton, which provide food for larger animals, such as fish and waterbirds. In turn, these larger animals are eaten by predators that live in the lake or around the water's edge.

Some lakes are so large that conditions for the lake dwellers are not the same in all parts of the lake. For this reason, biologists divide most lakes into three zones: the profundal zone, the limnetic zone, and the littoral zone.

The profundal zone

The profundal zone is the deepest part of the lake, just above the thick mud lining the bottom of the lake. There is little light or oxygen at this level. Most inhabitants of the profundal zone are small. Tiny algae and insect larvae provide food for slightly larger animals, such as mussels and worms.

In some large lakes, the profundal zone is very far down. For example, Lake Baikal in southeastern Siberia is the world's deepest lake, reaching 5712 ft (1741 m). This lake contains 20 percent of all the liquid freshwater on the planet. It is home to over a thousand types of unique creatures, which are found nowhere else. One of the strangest of these is a small, pinkish fish called the golomyanka. It lives at an amazing depth of 4595 ft (1400 m) and cannot survive being removed from the lake – it simply dissolves whenever it is taken out of the water.

The limnetic zone

High above the profundal zone is the limnetic zone. This is the top layer of water at the surface of the lake, which receives plenty of sunlight and oxygen. Thousands of microorganisms live in the limnetic zone.

Larger animals in this zone have adaptations to allow them to live here. Since the limnetic zone consists of open water, away from the edges and the bed below, the creatures here have to be able to float in the water or to swim well. Fish such as trout have a buoyant swim bladder in their body. This is filled with gas and prevents the fish from sinking. Other animals, such as frogs, grebes, otters, and turtles, are strong swimmers and

▼ Plants commonly found in the littoral zone include cattails, pondweed, reeds, and water lilies. Living in shallow waters near the shoreline, these large plants receive abundant oxygen, sunlight, and nutrients. They also help to create a habitat for other organisms – they provide an area of quiet water where fine mud settles and more delicate creatures can live without being battered by waves. Some fish, such as the stickleback, spend their entire lives in the littoral zone.

spend much of their time feeding on fish and insects in the middle of the lake. In some shallow lakes, larger animals, such as hippos, graze on aquatic plants while wallowing in the cooling waters.

The littoral zone

The littoral zone is the shallow area around the edge of the lake. This is the only part of the lake where sunlight can reach right to the bottom of the water, allowing rooted plants, such as cattails, pondweeds, reeds, and water lilies, to thrive. Dense clumps of these plants, growing up out of the lake or floating on the surface of the water, create a habitat for other organisms. These plants provide food, shelter, and breeding grounds for amphibians, birds, fish, insects, reptiles, and snails. Some fish, such as sticklebacks (family *Gasterosteidae*), spend their whole life in the littoral zone; others, such as Northern pike (*Esox*

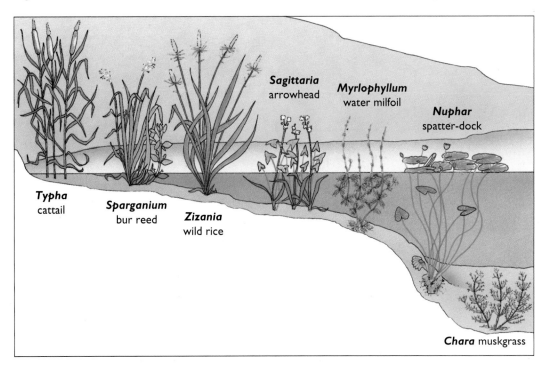

Sagittaria arrowhead

Myrlophyllum water milfoil

Nuphar spatter-dock

Typha cattail

Sparganium bur reed

Zizania wild rice

Chara muskgrass

appear during the rainy season and dry up completely during the long, dry months. Ponds are also more likely to freeze over during the harsh winter weather.

Rivers and streams

By contrast to lakes and ponds, rivers and streams consist of flowing water. They run from high ground to low ground, eventually running into lakes or the ocean. Some rivers can be particularly fast-flowing, with waters that churn up rocks and stones from the riverbed. Pacific salmon (*Oncorhynchus* spp.) have to be particularly good swimmers, because they spend the last weeks of their life swimming upstream (against the current) to reach their breeding grounds.

Rivers are divided into slow- and fast-moving zones. Each zone is host to its own particular animals. In the deep and fast-moving sections, fish such as barbel (*Barbus barbus*) and dace (family *Cyprinidae*) are found. Further down, in the murky

lucius), breed here, then swim out to the limnetic zone to feed.

Differences between lakes and ponds

Very few ponds have a profundal zone. Ponds are generally smaller and shallower than lakes, and all the water in most areas of a pond receives plenty of light and oxygen. As a result, ponds can support plants and animals throughout all parts of the water. As well as being much shallower and smaller than lakes, many ponds are also shorter-lived. They might

▲ *The European pond terrapin lives in freshwater ponds in southern Europe. Many other animals take advantage of pond habitats. Frogs and newts, mollusks such as water snails, birds such as ducks, and many insects make their homes in these environments.*

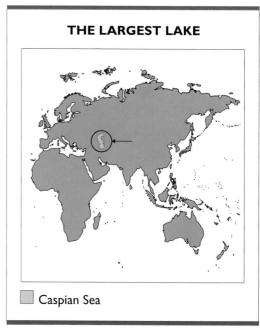

THE LARGEST LAKE

☐ Caspian Sea

waters of the lower reaches of the river, sunfish (*Lepomis gibbosas*) suck up the tiny invertebrates (spineless animals) that burrow in the mud or lodge themselves in the cracks and crevices of the riverbed. Snapping turtles (*Chelydra serpentina*) are also to be found here, preying on unwary fish that swim too close to their gaping mouth. Some animals, such as blackfly larvae, snails, and limpets, have special hooks or suckers that they use to hang on to rocks or plants so that they are not washed away by the current.

Many colorful wild plants, such as buttercups, cattails, and Water hyacinths, decorate the fertile banks of rivers and streams. Animals abound here, making their homes in the lush vegetation, or burrowing into the riverbanks themselves. Riverside inhabitants include alligators, bullfrogs, muskrats, and turtles, and birds, such as egrets, herons, and storks.

Estuaries

Estuaries occur where rivers and streams meet the ocean, forming bays and marshy inlets. They contain a mixture of freshwater and salt water. This is a particularly nutritious environment, with the water containing food particles from both the sea and the rivers. This kind of habitat can support a huge array of plants and animals, including aquatic worms, algae, barnacles, crabs, mangroves, marsh grasses, mudskippers, oysters, shrimps, and snails. When the tide goes out, wading birds, such as oystercatchers, and seabirds, such as gulls and terns, descend upon the estuary, feeding on the many creatures that litter the exposed mud.

The problem of pollution

Most of the world's lakes, rivers, and estuaries are threatened by pollution. For example, chemicals leak into the water when they are discharged from waste-water treatment plants and factories or when they run off surrounding farmland. These substances cause an overgrowth of algae. The algae use up the oxygen in the water, suffocating the other animals, plants, and microorganisms. As a result, the number of many freshwater animals, such as mussels and salmon, is declining.

▶ *The Sharptooth catfish has special whiskers, called barbels, around its mouth. It uses the barbels to probe the thick mud lining the bottom of the murky, oxygen-poor lake. It sucks up organic material through its gaping mouth.*

KEY FACTS

- **Largest lake in the world**
  The Caspian Sea (which is a lake and not a sea at all), covering an area of 152,239 sq miles (394,300 km²)

- **Deepest lake in the world**
  Lake Baikal in southeastern Siberia, which reaches a depth of 5712 ft (1741 m)

- **Longest river in the world**
  The Nile River, which stretches 4180 miles (6726 km) from Uganda to Egypt

- **Typical lake inhabitants**
  Beavers, catfish, cattails, dragonflies, ducks, frogs, grebes, mussels, otters, reeds, trout, turtles, water lilies, water striders

- **Typical river inhabitants**
  Alligators, bullfrogs, Caddis fly larvae, chub, eels, herons, muskrats, salmon, snails, Snapping turtles, storks

- **Typical estuary inhabitants**
  Barnacles, cockles, curlews, gulls, lugworms, shrimps, oystercatchers

See also **Alga, Cattail, Dragonfly, Eel, Frog, Grebe, Heron, Snail, Turtle, Water lily**

Lamprey

The lamprey and its close relative the hagfish make up one of the three main groups of fish, the jawless fish. These are very basic fish without bones; instead of bones their bodies are strengthened by cartilage (a firm, elastic material such as that found in the human nose).

The lamprey looks like an eel. It has slimy skin without scales and its fins are in a line down the center of the body. It has only one nostril, which is located in the middle of its head. There are about 40 species of lamprey, most of which live in the northern hemisphere. Some species are

NATURAL HABITAT

☐ Sea lamprey

found only in fresh water: others, such as the Sea lamprey, migrate from fresh water to salt water – they live in the sea but travel to rivers and lakes to breed (spawn).

Bloodsucking fish

Except for a group known as the brook lampreys, all lampreys are parasites that live on the blood and tissues of other fish. The lamprey feeds by attaching itself to the prey fish (the host) with its suckering mouth, then rasping away the scales, skin, and flesh, and sucking the blood. Sometimes the host fish loses all of its body fluids in this way. The lamprey's mouth contains special glands that produce chemicals to prevent the blood of the host fish from clotting so that the blood does not stop flowing. As a result the host fish may die following an attack by a lamprey. Fish that are attacked may also die because bacteria or fungi enter their wounds and cause infection.

Where lampreys are found in large numbers they may be a serious threat to

▲ *This Brook lamprey shows off its extraordinary mouth. It is a sucking circle containing many small teeth and a rasping tongue that works rather like a grater. This species is unusual because it remains in fresh water all its life, rather than returning to the sea after breeding.*

▶ *The Sea lamprey (and other species) latch onto a host fish and may continue to feed on its body fluids until it dies.*

local fishing industries. For example at one time the lampreys that live in the Great Lakes caused enormous damage to the populations of lake trout and other commercial and sports fish. By controlling the number of lampreys, other species have increased in number again.

Worm-like young

Adult lampreys spawn in rivers. They are strong swimmers, and migrating lampreys begin to move out of the seas during the winter. The males migrate first and by spring have arrived at their nesting sites, which are usually far up the river. As soon as they reach their destination they start building their nests on the stony river bottom. When the females arrive they help the males.

The lampreys make nests by removing pebbles from the riverbed with their sucking mouths; both male and female will work together to move a large pebble or a small stone. The pebbles are moved downstream and used to make a barrier. This creates a hollow in the riverbed upstream from the dam and this is where the female lays her eggs. After spawning both the male and female lampreys die.

The tiny eggs hatch about two weeks after they are laid. The young, called larvae, are blind and look like small worms. Their mouths are surrounded by fleshy tentacles. The larvae look so unlike the adult lampreys that at one time scientists thought they were an entirely different species, and called them ammocoetes. Some people still use this name for them.

The ammocoetes burrow in the sand or mud of the riverbank and come out at night to feed on small particles of plant and animal food, which they filter from the water. They spend three to five years in this way and, when they are 4-5 in (10-12.5 cm) long, they change into adults. Their mouths develop into funnel-shaped sucking tubes and the eyes grow larger. The Sea lamprey becomes silver in color before migrating out to sea.

In spite of their name, the river lampreys also migrate to the sea, where they parasitize fish as well as eating various mollusks, crustaceans, and worms.

KEY FACTS

- **Name**
  Sea lamprey
  (*Petromyzon marinus*)

- **Range**
  Atlantic coast of North America from Labrador south to Florida; Iceland and the northwestern coasts of Africa and Europe; occasionally found in the Baltic and Mediterranean Seas

- **Habitat**
  Seas at depths of up to 1640 ft (500 m) and often near mouths of rivers; most of their life is spent in fresh water

- **Appearance**
  35 in (90cm) long; an eel-like body, dark yellowish-brown with black mottling, underside grayish; the body is slimy; no scales; round mouth

- **Food**
  Parasitic

- **Breeding**
  Adults move to rivers in the spring; females lay up to 200,000 eggs from May-June; young fish live in the mud for about 6 years then migrate to the sea

- **Status**
  Widespread

505

Larch

The larch is a conifer (a woody plant with cones). It is related to the evergreen cedar, fir, pine, and spruce and, like them, bears both male and female cones (woody structures that contain the male or female reproductive cells). Unlike them, however, larches are deciduous; that is, they shed their leaves in the fall.

There are nine species of larch (*Larix* spp.), which belong to the *Pinaceae* family.

▲ *The Western larch (Larix occidentalis) is found across wide areas of North America. During the fall, the leaves turn from green to yellow before they drop, covering the woodland floor below.*

Larches live in the moderately cool (temperate) and subarctic regions of Asia, Europe, and North America. Most grow best on well-drained soils. One species, Sikkim larch (*Larix griffithiana*), is found only in the Himalayas in Asia.

Christmas-tree conifers

The young larch has the distinctive, conical, Christmas-tree shape common to most conifers. Its bark is scaly on young trees, becoming thick and deeply grooved as the tree gets older. The leaves – which look more like short needles – are pale or bright green in spring and summer, turning yellow in the fall. On new growth, the leaves are arranged in spirals; on older twigs between 10 and 40 soft, light-green needles are arranged in clusters.

Larches are tall trees – the European larch (*Larix decidua*) may grow up to 140 ft (about 42 m) high. This species is native to

NATURAL HABITAT

☐ Original habitat of European larch

KEY FACTS

● **Name**

European larch
(*Larix decidua*)

● **Range**

Native to central and
eastern Europe; now
widely planted in
northern and central
Europe and North
America

● **Habitat**

Mountains and
cultivated forests

● **Appearance**

Deciduous (they lose
their leaves in fall),
cone-bearing plant
with scaly, gray-black
bark; pale-green
needles ⅗-1⅕ in
(1.5-3 cm) long,
spirally arranged on
one-year shoots;
clusters of 25 to 40
needles on older
twigs; purplish-red,
oval, female cones
about ⅘-1⅖ in
(2-3.5 cm) long and
become brown and
woody; male cones
yellow; light-brown
seeds to ⅙ in (4 mm)

● **Life cycle**

Perennial

● **Uses**

Timber; source of
turpentine; bark
contains tannin, used
to tan leather

● **Status**

Common

the Alps and the mountains in central and eastern Europe. Today, however, the European larch is cultivated throughout northern and central Europe and has also been introduced to North America.

The most widely distributed native North America larch is the Eastern larch (*Larix laricina*). It is also known by the native American name "tamarack." Eastern larches have gray to reddish-brown bark and take between 100 and 200 years to reach their mature height of 40-100 ft (12-30 m). A slightly taller species, the Western larch (*Larix occidentalis*), occurs in British Columbia, Canada, and the U.S. states of Idaho, Montana, Oregon, and Washington.

A useful tree

Larch wood is strong, heavy, and hard. It has a wide range of industrial applications, notably in ship construction and to make mine timbers, railroad ties, and telephone poles. The bark of the European larch produces a clear, resinous oil known as Venetian turpentine, which is used to remove paint.

The larch is also widely valued for its natural beauty. Several species are grown in the United States as

▶ **At first, the female cones of the European larch are red or purple. They mature to become brown and woody.**

ornamental trees, especially the Japanese larch (*Larix kaempferi*), which is used as a landscaping tree, and a cultivated variety of European larch called *pendula,* which is used in eastern states for reforestation.

A wide distribution

Today some of the most extensive and productive larch forests are found in Belgium, the Northwest Territories in Canada, Japan, Korea, Poland, northern Russia, Switzerland, and Alaska and Montana in the United States. Although originally a tree of the northern hemisphere, the larch was imported into South America, where it is now particularly well-established in the mountainous forests of Patagonia in southern Argentina.

One of the greatest natural threats to the larch tree is the larvae of the Larch sawfly (*Pristophora erichsonii*). This destructive pest has destroyed large areas of larch forests in England and Scotland.

Lemming

Lemmings are fascinating animals that live in the freezing snow of the Arctic tundra. They are small rodents with stout bodies, short tails, blunt muzzles, and small eyes and ears. They are closely related to voles and are found only in the northern hemisphere, from Canada and some of the northern states of the U.S., across the Arctic wastes to the Alaskan Peninsula, Siberia, Russia, and the Scandinavian countries of northern Europe.

Like other creatures that live in very cold conditions, lemmings must be able to survive the long, dark Arctic winters. They do not hibernate, nor do they store up extra layers of fat on their bodies to protect them from freezing temperatures. They do, however, have long, heavy fur coats that are waterproof. And they are able to live under the snow, which acts as insulation against the cold when they tunnel into it.

Surviving the Arctic winter

Two types of lemming have evolved additional features for living in the snow. In the Norway lemming, the claw on the first toe of each of the forefeet is flattened and larger than the other claws, making an excellent instrument for digging. The Collared lemming is even more specialized. In the winter the third and fourth claws of the forefeet become enlarged as a thick, horny shield develops under the permanent claws. These special "snow claws" are probably used for shoveling the snow. They fall off in the spring. The Collared lemming is also the only rodent that molts during the fall and grows a pure white coat for the winter.

Lemmings feed on various kinds of plant material. What they eat depends largely on what is available at that time of year. In the summer, some prefer the stems and leaves of green plants, while others

KEY FACTS

● **Name**
Collared, Greenland collared, or Arctic lemming (*Dicrostonyx groenlandicus*)

● **Range**
Northern N. America

● **Habitat**
Arctic tundra

● **Appearance**
Brown or gray in summer with a black stripe down the middle of the back and a white collar; pure white in winter; head and body length 5-6 in (13-16 cm), with a tail of $\frac{1}{3}$-$\frac{1}{2}$ in (1-2 cm)

● **Food**
Grasses, berries in summer, twigs in winter

● **Breeding**
2-3 litters per year, each with 1-7 young

● **Status**
Common

◄ *The gray summer coat of this Collared lemming blends in with the rocky background. In winter it turns white to blend with the snow.*

prefer mosses or roots and bulbs. In the winter many lemmings eat twigs and any grasses they can find beneath the snow. They feed at night as well as in the day, but are most active at dawn and dusk.

Breeding can take place at any time of year. Under normal conditions there are one to three litters a year, each with one to nine young. However, every few years (usually every four) the number of lemmings in the population becomes very high, resulting in a dramatic shortage of resources. The most famous and well-reported example of the consequences of this is seen in the Norway lemming.

Mass migrations

The Norway lemming (*Lemmus lemmus*) is a species that lives in Norway, Sweden, and Finland. It is usually found in mountainous regions, above the tree line (the line above which trees cannot grow). In normal years these lemmings move about between the tree line and the line of permanent snow in a controlled way, searching for food. But when there is a population explosion (a "lemming year") the pressure on food sources becomes greater and the lemmings must move farther afield to feed. They then begin to migrate haphazardly in all directions, leaving their usual habitat and, even traveling down the mountain into the river valleys.

Outside the breeding season, the lemming is a solitary creature and cannot tolerate the presence of other lemmings. In a lemming year, as the number of lemmings increases, individuals become stressed. This, and the shortage of food, can result in panic. Faced with a body of

water or some other obstacle, the lemmings can only move forward or stay where they are.

Many lemmings die of starvation or exhaustion brought about by stress. Some others drown when they have to cross lakes and rivers. Lemmings can swim, but they cannot survive in water over long periods of time. Because of the high death rate at this time, the number of lemmings falls as rapidly and dramatically as it rose. The population density then returns to "normal" and the cycle begins again.

The Norway lemming is not the only species to undertake long migrations when their population increases. Brown lemmings and Collared lemmings also have "lemming years" and migrations, but not to the same extent.

▲ *This Norway lemming seems to be surrounded by plenty of space and plant food. However, during a "lemming year," the shortage of food and space to live can be disastrous for these animals, causing them to do anything to escape – usually with fatal results.*

NATURAL HABITAT

Greenland collared lemming

Lemur

The lemur is a strange-looking animal that belongs to a group of mammals known as the prosimians, or "pre-monkeys." Like the monkey and the ape (which are known as simians) the lemur is a primate. However, it is a very basic primate, only halfway to being an ape, which is reflected in the German word for lemur: *Halb-Affen*, meaning "half ape."

Lemurs are found only in one small part of the world, on the island of Madagascar in the Indian Ocean, off the southeastern coast of Africa. The island is remarkable for the number of unusual wild animals that live there and are found nowhere else in the world. How the lemurs and other rare animals arrived on Madagascar is a mystery that still puzzles some scientists.

All shapes and sizes

Lemurs are found on almost every part of Madagascar, mainly in forests but also in areas of dry scrub. They range in size from the small Dwarf and Mouse lemurs, which are rarely over 12 in (30 cm) long, to the indri and sifaka. The indri, the largest lemur, grows to a length of 30 in (75 cm). The aye-aye is a close relative of the true lemurs.

The Dwarf and Mouse lemurs have short, pointed faces and long, fairly bushy tails. Their fur on the upperparts is reddish to gray, and white or yellow on the underparts. Both Mouse and Dwarf lemurs spend almost all their time in trees, although the Dwarf species will climb down to the ground if necessary

in order to reach a tree that lies some distance away. Sometimes the Mouse lemur hunts on the forest floor for beetles and other small insects.

The lemurs are divided into five distinct groups. These are the true lemurs, the Ring-tailed lemur, the variegated or ruffed lemurs, the Brown lemur, and the gentle

▼ *Once a baby Ring-tailed lemur is a few days old, it can move from its mother's belly onto her back, where it clings to her fur. She carries the baby around as she forages.*

lemurs, which are very rare and found in only a few places on the island.

The Ring-tailed lemur

The Ring-tailed lemur is a true lemur. Like other lemurs, it has mobile fingers and a thumb on its hands, which are suitable for grasping branches and fruit. The arms are much longer than the legs. In many ways it is similar to a cat (its Latin name is *Lemur catta*); it is about the same size, has soft gray fur and its cry sounds very much like "meow." However, the muzzle is pointed, like that of a fox, with bare skin around the nostrils.

The Ring-tailed lemur is active during the day and spends much time on the ground with other members of the troop. (Many other lemurs are active at night or at dusk and spend the day quietly, basking in the sun.) A troop may contain about 12 individuals. Unlike many other

animals, the female lemur is actually dominant over the male.

The Ring-tailed lemur is particularly easy to identify by its distinctive black and white ringed tail, which is longer than the length of the head and body combined. It holds its tail upright when it is on the ground, which acts as a visual signal to other members of the group. Like all true lemurs the Ring-tailed has scent glands on its body that it uses to mark territory, and males also use them to deter rival males.

Caring for the young

The mating season for the true lemurs lasts from April to June. The single young is born 4½ months later, somewhere between August and November. In some species, for example the Ruffed, Dwarf, and Mouse lemurs, the young lemur is born naked and not fully developed. Immediately after its birth its mother places it in a nest of leaves. The Ruffed lemur makes a leafy nest in the fork of a tree and lines it with fur she pulls from her sides. The Ring-tailed lemur gives birth to a fully developed baby, however, which clings to her belly for a few days before moving around to her back.

◀ *Most true lemurs, like the Ring-tailed lemur shown here, live in trees. They move about mainly on all four legs and are adept at leaping a distance of several feet.*

KEY FACTS

- **Name**
  Ring-tailed lemur
  (*Lemur catta*)

- **Range**
  Madagascar

- **Habitat**
  Open, scrubby bush and forest

- **Appearance**
  Gray with lighter limbs and belly and white areas on the tips of the feet and ears; a very long tail with well defined black and white rings; yellow eyes; the length of head and body is 15-18 in (39-46 cm), with a tail of 22-25 in (56-63 cm)

- **Food**
  Leaves and fruit

- **Breeding**
  Single (sometimes 2) young born August-November

- **Status**
  Threatened

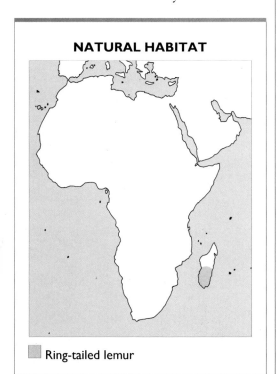

NATURAL HABITAT

Ring-tailed lemur

Index

Page numbers in **boldface** type show full articles